JULIA GOODFELLOW-SMITH

111 PLACES IN WORCESTERSHIRE THAT YOU SHOULDN'T MISS

111

Photographs by Julia & Mike Goodfellow-Smith

emons:

To Les. I miss you.

Cäcilienstraße 48, 50667 Köln
info@emons-verlag.de

Layout: Conny Laue, based on a design by Lübbeke | Naumann | Thoben
Maps: altancicek.design, www.altancicek.de
Basic cartographical information from Openstreetmap,
© OpenStreetMap-Mitwirkende, OdbL
QR code notice: External content is provided via Google Maps.
Google's privacy policy applies.
Edited by Tania Taylor
Printing and binding: sourc-e GmbH
Printed in Europe 2026
ISBN 978-3-7408-2842-4

Guidebooks for Locals & Experienced Travellers
Join us in uncovering new places around the world at
www.111places.com

FOREWORD

If 'Worcestershire' conjures up thoughts of a middle-of-the-road county in Middle England, it's time to think again. This is where the Romans came to manufacture salt from its saline springs. This is where the Saxons established great centres of monastic learning. This is where great battles have been fought, moving the country towards democracy.

Parts of the county were crucial centres of manufacturing during the Industrial Revolution, parts fed the growing urban centres of that era, and several towns provided refuge as early tourist destinations.

More recently, research conducted here tipped the balance of World War II in the Allies' favour. Ongoing research is teaching the world about deep space.

This is where Sir Edward Elgar composed, and J. R. R. Tolkien and C. S. Lewis were inspired to write. This is where Jenny Lind, 'The Swedish Nightingale', sang, and John 'Bonzo' Bonham from Led Zeppelin learned to play drums. This is a county with music festivals and theatres galore, keeping the cultural tradition alive.

Worcestershire's rolling hills are covered in meadows ablaze with poppies and orchids in summer, abuzz with moths and butterflies, and home to skylarks, sounding for all the world like space invaders high overhead. In the evenings, it is bats and owls that take over the skies. But the wildlife is not all native; here, you can also sleep with lions and commune with hippos.

Here, you will find innovation, exciting activities and more gentle pursuits. Here, you will be surprised, inspired and delighted, whether you already know the county well or are visiting for the first time. Having lived in Worcestershire for over a decade, I thought I knew the county inside out, but I have discovered so much more while researching this book – and fallen even more in love with this beautiful, exciting and vibrant county. I hope you do, too.

FAVOURITE TOURS

Most of the places in this book are spread out around the county. However, there are a few concentrations where it is possible to visit several on a fairly short walk.

GREAT MALVERN

On this two-mile walk, there are 16 places to visit. Malvern is built on a steep hill, but there are plenty of places to rest. Start at Great Malvern station ch. 59. The Technology Station ch. 68 is next to the ticket office. Head up to Avenue Road, cross and look right to see The Worm ch. 71. Turn uphill, walking between some marvellous trees ch. 64. Pass Elmslie House ch. 56 on the left, then take the next left and turn right into Priory Park. Cross Swan Pool ch. 67 and turn left around the theatre, passing the George Bernard Shaw Mulberry ch. 58. Continue uphill into the priory churchyard, where you will find Anne Darwin's grave ch. 52 and some gas lamps ch. 57. The Green Man misericord ch. 60 resides inside the priory, along with many other treasures. Continue uphill again (you're almost at the top) to exit the churchyard. Take a quick detour up and to the left to see the bird sculptures in Rose Bank Gardens ch. 66 before heading onto Bellevue Island to fill your water bottle at Malvhina ch. 63. Down the steps, turn left uphill (sorry!) to visit the Bluebird Tea Rooms ch. 54, a favourite haunt of Elgar. A few more paces uphill will take you to Edith Walk, where you will find the world's tiniest theatre ch. 70. Next, weave your way downhill to Malvern Cube ch. 62. From here, turn south, then left on Church Street and right on Imperial Road to see the Binidome ch. 53 on the way back to the station.

ALONG THE RIVER IN WORCESTER

This tour begins at Worcester Foregate Street railway station and is just over three miles. Take the path along the left side of the railway arches, past Method Roastery ch. 107, and continue until you see a honey-coloured building on your left – The Hive ch. 105. Bear left down to the river, where the route continues to the left. Once you have passed the road bridge, the path becomes tranquil, except during swan feeding time ch. 109. The cathedral is ahead; when you reach its water gate by the ferry steps, look left to see the flood markers ch. 102. Continue along the river for a while, past Diglis Island and Locks. Cross the river on the high pedestrian bridge and turn right to head back upstream. Almost immediately, you will reach the portrait bench ch. 101. Past the weir, Diglis Fish Pass ch. 100 has a fish viewing gallery. Continue upstream until the road bridge, where you can cross the river and find your way back to the station.

DROITWICH SPA

This four-mile walk circles clockwise through Droitwich Spa. It starts at the lido car park, although you could travel by train and follow Salwarpe Road to the canal (cross and turn right to join the route). From the lido car park, head past the pool and tennis courts and into the park. As you progress, you will see St Peter's Fields conifer and pine arboretum on your left ch. 22. Turn right in front of the church to exit the park on the west side, continuing ahead to Worcester Road. Here, turn left until you see the Church of the Sacred Heart on your right ch. 20. It looks quite plain from the outside, but head inside for a real treat. On exiting, turn left onto Worcester Road, then take the first left onto Old Coach Road. Chawson Pleck (fourth right) will take you over the railway. Continue in the same direction to the canal, where the route crosses and turns right to follow the towpath to Vines Park. Here, you will find the Salt Worker ch. 21, celebrating what was once an important industry in the town. Continue to Bromsgrove Road, where the route turns right, to return to the start.

111 PLACES

Scan here for
the digital map

1 Alfrick Community Café

Hitting the sweet spot

For cyclists and ramblers seeking a sweet treat or a warming drink on their day out, the Alfrick & Lulsley Community Shop and Café is an icon of good hospitality. It has bike racks, tables outside in a sheltered garden, and space inside in case drying off is the order of the day, with friendly volunteers offering a warm welcome. For locals, the café provides a place to meet their neighbours and catch up on village news. The homemade cakes are legendary, and the café also serves a small selection of savouries, such as sandwiches. Of course, the café would not be successful these days if it didn't also serve excellent coffee.

Many villages have lost facilities as driving has become the dominant means of transport. Alfrick's pub closed in the year 2000. The village shop and post office remained open for another 11 years, until its owners retired. Concerned villagers immediately swung into action, and the community shop and café run by volunteers opened less than 12 months later. The shop has approximately 60 to 70 volunteers, which is almost 10 per cent of the population. This indicates how important the facility is to the village. The shop offers everyday groceries, locally produced food and drink, and a post office counter that provides postal and banking services.

As this is a community-owned asset, surplus profits are donated to local projects. In recent years, the earnings from the Alfrick & Lulsley Show, held on the first Saturday in September, have been combined with those of the shop, resulting in donations of around £10,000 a year.

What an achievement for a small village to have created a hub of community activity that is well loved by locals and visitors alike, and continues to go from strength to strength. For those arriving from afar, there's a good-sized car park. Groups are welcome, but please phone ahead if you are a large group, to avoid a long wait.

ADDRESS Alfrick, WR6 5HJ TIP If you like the idea of a wild swim and sauna before your coffee and cake, Escape to the Lake is less than three miles to the east (www.escapetothelake.co.uk).

2 Mortsafe

Solving a grave issue

After the collapse of the Roman Empire in the 5th century, the church outlawed the dissection of human bodies. Those who wished to study anatomy had to rely on old texts and animal dissection. Whilst the practice of medicine remained mainly in the hands of religious communities, this edict was abided by. However, by the 14th century, medical practice had spread into the wider community, and dissection of human cadavers was being performed, with the bodies sourced by the students themselves. Almost immediately, entrepreneurs filled the gap in the market by supplying bodies, which were sometimes sourced from recently buried coffins. Across Europe, governments resolved this issue by supplying bodies themselves, with the added benefit of avoiding burial costs.

However, in England, the authorities did not react in the same way. Instead, they restricted the supply of dead bodies to those of executed criminals. Not only did this mean that demand outstripped supply, but also that no one wanted a family member's body to be used in this way, as it would make them look like a criminal. In response, the body-snatching business became highly lucrative. There was no way to preserve the cadavers back then, so a constant supply was needed, giving the bodysnatchers the upper hand in any negotiations with the medical establishment.

They became so busy that the public started to react. Sometimes, graves were booby-trapped. Sometimes, members of the family, or the community at large, took on watch duties until the body was sufficiently decomposed to be of no interest to the bodysnatchers. Others used a mortsafe – an iron cage – to make it exceedingly difficult for the bodysnatchers to do their worst.

Although there is no gravestone, this mortsafe, because of its size, is believed to be protecting a child's coffin. At least one body was allowed to rest in peace.

ADDRESS Dowles Graveyard, Dowles Road, Bewdley, DY12 2RG **TIP** A public footpath runs north-east from the graveyard to the River Severn. Turn left along the river to see another curiosity – the piers of Dowles Bridge, which once carried trains on the Wyre Forest Line.

3 Safari Lodges

Pick your own adventure

What do images of safari parks conjure up for you? Cars creeping along, nose to tail like a baby elephant laboriously following its mother? Crowds of people peering like meerkats for the best views?

Have you ever wondered what happens when the throng of visitors leaves at the end of the day? Do the animals chat to each other in the dark? Or does the park descend into silence? If you were sleeping there, would you wake with your heart thumping to the sound of a lion's roar? If you did, what would you do then? Hunker down under your duvet, knowing you're safe and sound, or tiptoe to your window or balcony and peer into the dark, hoping to spot the source of the sound?

At West Midlands Safari Park, you can find out the answers to all of these questions by staying overnight in one of their safari lodges. Take your pick of the enclosure you would like your windows or balcony to overlook. Would you prefer to see a tiger padding past your window, a cheetah slinking through the grass, or a lion majestically watching you eat your dinner? Or perhaps you'd like to experience elephants spraying themselves with water or hippos submerging themselves in the pool outside your lodge? Maybe you'd like to spend your breakfast time communing with giraffes or laughing at the antics of the red pandas.

Staying in a safari lodge will make you feel like an intrepid explorer and a VIP all wrapped together. After hours, when other visitors have left the park, guests are treated to exclusive wildlife experiences. They can wander freely through the pedestrian areas, taking their time and stopping to gaze at the animals at will. Cinematic views of the animals walking right past your windows, at dawn and dusk, add to the magic and the sense that this is a once-in-a-lifetime experience. Although it doesn't have to be – there's always another night and another lodge to tempt you…

ADDRESS West Midlands Safari Park, Spring Grove, Bewdley, DY12 1LF, www.safari-lodges.co.uk **TIP** If you prefer hands-on animal encounters, Little Owl Farm Park between Kidderminster and Worcester offers petting opportunities as well as talks and energetic activities for children (www.littleowlfarmpark.co.uk).

4 The Fold

A breath of fresh air

The Fold embraces visitors with its aura of tranquillity. Whether you arrive frazzled or feeling zen, you will leave with a gladdened heart, for this not-for-profit is all about connecting – with yourself, with others and with the natural world.

Start your visit with a walk around the nature trails. Follow the shady, tree-lined track down past the campsite for Green and Away, the summer tented events space. Once in the meadow below, turn left at the reservoir towards the River Teme. Keep an eye out for Common Blue butterflies as you cross the meadow, and kingfishers and otters down by the river before rising again, to join the railway trail. This follows the line of the long-defunct Worcester to Leominster railway and will return you to the track, where you can follow another loop around The Tank – the upper reservoir. Here, you can enjoy a picnic while watching the dragonflies hunting around the lake or buzzards quartering the sky above.

When you have finished exploring, a treat awaits you in the old farm buildings. The café serves delicious vegetarian food, including cake, many of the ingredients grown organically on the farm. It's a great place to linger and soak up the atmosphere before exploring again – this time, the artists' studios. Some organise workshops so you can learn a skill; others sell their lovingly hand-crafted wares.

Alternatively, you can book yourself a choice of natural therapies, which are offered in an ancient building that exudes the calm of the Shire horses that were once stabled there.

During the week, The Fold usually has a gentle hum of activity. On weekends, it is busier, with music events and monthly markets that align with a sustainability ethos. However, the aura of tranquillity is not lost; it is built into the fabric of the place, the very structure of the buildings, and infects all who spend some time in its embrace.

ADDRESS The Fold, Bransford, WR6 5JB, +44 (0) 1886 833633, www.thefold.org.uk, reception@thefold.org.uk **TIP** If you like eating organic food but can't get to The Fold, try Greenlink Organic Foods store and café on Graham Road in Great Malvern (www.facebook.com/greenlinkmalvern).

5 Heart Burial

Home is where the heart is

Conflict in the Middle East is not new. Neither are wars that seem to rumble on forever. In the 11th century, Muslims ruled Jerusalem and the Holy Land. After the fall of the Carolingian Empire, the Catholic Church had lost power as Europe degenerated into squabbling tribes.

Amidst all this, a new social class arose. Known as 'knights' in English, members of this class were closely connected to horses and lived by a code of 'chivalry' (from the French for horse – 'cheval'). Their code of conduct had three main tenets: a duty of loyalty – most strongly felt towards family; a duty of largesse – to share the spoils of war with those they were loyal to; and a duty of prowess – to fight fair, which included the idea that noblemen should be captured for ransom, not killed. Essentially, they played war games focused on generating wealth for their nearest and dearest.

Pope Urban II spotted an opportunity: a holy crusade to restore Jerusalem and the Holy Land to Christianity would unite the knights, give them a common purpose, and strengthen the Catholic Church. In 1095, the First Crusade began. And for the next two centuries, waves of crusades were fought in the Holy Land, thousands of people were slaughtered, and many ransoms paid before the crusaders lost their final outpost in 1291.

This tomb is thought to contain the heart of Sir Nicholas de Mitton, a local knight who lost his life in the crusades. It was difficult to preserve a body killed on a foreign battlefield and transport it home, particularly as travel was slow, and refrigeration was not an option, so it was not unusual to return a small part of the body to the person's home parish. And, of course, the heart suggests a love of home and a noble death, serving the god of love. Rather ironic, really, given the number of people who died in this quest for power, which had nothing to do with love at all.

ADDRESS St Giles Church, Church Street, Bredon, GL20 7LF **TIP** The National Trust's Bredon Barn, built in the 14th century, is within a stone's throw to the west of the church (www.nationaltrust.org.uk), and it is usually open from dawn to dusk.

6 John Clarke Walk

A proliferation of poppies

The common poppy, also known as the corn- or field poppy, has symbolised blood and new life for millennia. Poppies thrive in disturbed soil and can be found wherever fields are tilled. During World War I, in the summer after bloody battles in which many lives were lost, these beautiful red flowers sprang from the soil, attracting clouds of butterflies and new life.

During World War II, the UK's food imports were disrupted, so agricultural production had to be increased. The following two decades were characterised by intensive herbicide use, which almost eradicated poppies from the British landscape.

By the 1980s, the British population was missing the sight of these delicate red flowers. Gardeners started to plant wildflower mixes that included poppy seeds, and the Kemerton Estate started to leave its field boundaries unplanted and untreated with herbicide. Luckily, poppies have a superpower. On average, each plant produces 17,000 seeds, and about one in six of those will remain dormant yet viable for decades. When herbicides were no longer used, the seeds sprang into life.

The work of the Kemerton Estate demonstrated how straightforward it was to restore biodiversity, and was instrumental in introducing the set-aside scheme into the European Commission's Common Agricultural Policy, which required farmers to leave strips of land around their arable fields for wildflowers and the wildlife they attract.

Now, the estate leaves several of its arable fields unplanted and untreated. This has resulted in a riotous eruption of red poppies, which is best seen between June and August. The John Clarke Walk, which is just shy of a mile long, follows public footpaths around and through these fields and commemorates the estate's conservation adviser. The route also crosses grassland with pyramidal orchids in May to June and wood pasture and woodland that brim with birdsong.

ADDRESS Public footpath starts at Oat Hill Cottage, Westmancote, GL20 7ES, www.explore.osmaps.com/route/31351728 **TIP** Kemerton and Bredon churchyards both have graves of those who lost their lives during the world wars (www.cwgc.org).

7 The Fleece Inn

15th-century budget housing

There's a reason that many traditional medieval longhouses have not survived. It's because they were cheap, thrown up to house newly freed people with little money. The bubonic plague that swept through the country several times in the 14th century, along with a climate change-induced famine, halved the population. The workforce shrank so much that it gave the remaining serfs – people tied to the Lord of the Manor and the land they farmed – bargaining power. Many were granted their freedom and started to be paid for their work, and, as much of the land was no longer economically viable for the lords to farm, ordinary people could buy parcels for themselves. This necessitated mass-produced, low-cost housing for these new landowners, a need that was met by wood-framed buildings like these.

In the intervening 600 years, most have disappeared, and Worcestershire hosts a particularly high concentration of those that remain. The Byrd family, who owned this farm, gradually accumulated wealth, generation by generation, and extended the original building into something more substantial.

In the 19th century, the Industrial Revolution led to massive population growth and, consequently, increased demand for food. However, it also led to cheap food imports. It was time to diversify. Henry Byrd started to import rum and, in 1848, opened the doors of his home to the public for the purpose of drinking ale. He called his public house the Fleece Inn, presumably as a nod to the wool trade that the farm had previously relied on.

Over time, the farm was sold, and all that remained was the pub, with enough land around it for a smallholding. The pub stayed in the family, run first by his wife Ann, then by his daughter Ann, followed by her daughter – also Ann! The final owner-licensee was her daughter, Lola, and on her death in 1977, she left the pub to the National Trust.

ADDRESS The Cross, Bretforton, Evesham, WR11 7JE, +44 (0) 1386 831173, www.thefleeceinn.co.uk, info@thefleeceinn.co.uk **TIP** If you love half-timbered buildings, the National Trust also looks after a 16th-century half-timbered dovecote at Hawford, WR3 7SG (www.nationaltrust.org.uk).

8 Broadway Tower

Lighthouse of learning

What did you collect as a child? Marbles? Stickers? Pokémon cards? By the time Sir Thomas Phillipps, Baronet of Middle Hill, was six years old, he had spent all of his pocket money on collecting books – 110 of them. What may have started as a harmless hobby became an obsession, and by the time he died, he owned 50,000 printed books and 60,000 manuscripts. He had not quite achieved his lifetime ambition of owning a copy of every book in the world, but he made an exceptionally good stab at it!

In 1818, Sir Thomas inherited the estate that included Broadway Tower. It was built by the 6th Earl of Coventry as a token of his love for his second wife, Lady Barbara, and formed part of the romantic landscape he commissioned around their main residence at Croome Court. Initially, the tower was used for entertaining, but its new owner decided to house a printing press there instead. Most of the manuscripts he owned had not been published, and he wanted to share the wisdom they contained. The Middle Hill Press was born, and printed versions of the manuscripts were soon being produced. Free copies were distributed to libraries, and the tower was likened to a lighthouse signalling hospitality to all 'pilgrims of learning'.

Unfortunately, Sir Thomas' beneficence did not seem to extend to his employees. In the 50 or so years of operation, Middle Hill Press went through 42 different printers, and it seems that the printers' accommodation in the tower was not always of a salubrious standard.

In 1863, Sir Thomas moved to Cheltenham. Consider the difficulty of moving house with a collection book numbering in the tens of thousands. It took two years to transport everything! Perhaps he would be surprised to learn that ownership of the tower has now passed on, and that it is open to the public to ensure its survival as an important landmark in both the physical and literary landscape.

ADDRESS Broadway, WR12 7LB, www.broadwaytower.co.uk TIP The Coventrys' main residence, Croome Court, and its surrounding parkland, is now owned by the National Trust and open to the public (www.nationaltrust.org.uk).

9 Fairy Village

A visitor's guide to noticing the nearly-seen

Do you have fairies living at the bottom of your garden? Have you noticed that they tend to be shy and difficult to spot, often steering clear of humans as other creatures do? Sometimes they choose to live at the top of trees, where they can relax in their gardens with their wild friends, away from prying human eyes, and slip between the realms of reality and fantasy at will. However, here in Broadway, the fairies have a special relationship with the Knight family, so they have built a village where they live in plain sight, at the bottom of the garden.

This means they can play with the youngest Knights and share stories and wisdom from other realms with the oldest Knights. As a public footpath runs through the garden, it also means that passing wanderers can be enchanted by their community, although the fairies themselves generally remain elusive to strangers.

Fairy magic means the allotment grows delicious vegetables all year, and that washing will dry on the line, whatever the weather. Does it extend to ensuring that fairies don't feel hungover, even when they have imbibed a little too much nectar in the Blue Butterfly Inn, while the younger fairies were playing on the slide outside?

If you allow yourself to be sprinkled with fairy dust as you enter the garden, who knows who you might see and what you might experience. Fairies are drawn to thresholds: visit at dawn, dusk, midwinter or midsummer. Walk slowly and carefully through the village, perhaps singing a song of invitation to raise their curiosity about this strange human. Look out for tiny changes in the world around you. It might become still, as though holding its breath, or brighter, somehow visually sharper than usual. And, if you are extremely lucky, you might just be rewarded with a glimmer of light, a flicker, a dart of movement in the corner of your vision – a fairy coming to say hello.

ADDRESS Take the footpath along the side of 1 Cheltenham Road, Broadway, WR12 7BY (the fairy village is about 50 yards down) **TIP** Fairies are often associated with springs. There are over 100 springs, wells and fountains on the Malvern Hills, and each year around May Bank Holiday, many of the wells are decorated (www.malvernspa.org).

10 Lygon Arms Pear Tree

Symbolic fruit

Worcestershire has a strong association with tree fruit, as it is one of the counties with the most apple and plum orchards in the country. It is also famous for its pears, and especially the Black Pear. Worcestershire County Cricket Club and Worcester Rugby Football Club both have three Black Pears on their crests, and in 2013, a design with three Black Pears won a competition for the new county flag, now seen fluttering from flagpoles across Worcestershire. The county council's coat of arms depicts a fruiting pear tree, too, although those pears are deep red to match the rest of its logo.

It is thought that pears were introduced to Worcestershire by the Normans. At the Battle of Agincourt in 1415, where English forces beat the French, despite having the odds seriously against them, the Worcestershire bowmen proudly carried banners that depicted a fruiting pear tree. By the 15th century, the city of Worcester was known for this fruit in particular. It is said that when Queen Elizabeth I visited Worcester in the 16th century, a pear tree was moved to the city gates to make the entrance more attractive. She was apparently so impressed with the tree that she decreed that the city's coat of arms should depict three pears. It now does – Black Pears.

Plenty of other people will have been impressed by the mature espaliered pear tree growing up the front of The Lygon Arms in Broadway. The tree easily reaches the window of the fourth storey of this historic Cotswold stone building. In spring, it is covered with blossom that floats along the high street like confetti, and in autumn, deep red pears drip from its branches, close in colour to the county crest. Trained up a south-facing wall, the tree will benefit from the heat retained by the stone when the sun shines on it, protecting it from frost in spring and helping the fruit to ripen towards the end of the summer.

ADDRESS High Street, Broadway, WR12 7DU, www.lygonarmshotel.co.uk
TIP Cider and perry from Barbourne Cider, brewed in Worcester from Worcestershire apples and pears, are served at The Plough at 23 Fish Street in Worcester.

11 Nuclear Bunker

Concrete courage

World War II did not end with peace, but with a nuclear arms race. The 'hot' war turned 'cold'. In just a few short years, the Soviet Union tested its first nuclear weapon, and it was not long before the threat of nuclear war grew.

Part of the preparations in Britain was a series of nuclear bunkers staffed by civilian volunteers, to report on levels of nuclear fallout should the worst happen. Members of the Royal Observer Corps met at this bunker for a couple of hours a week to train. In the event of an escalation of tension and a high likelihood of a nuclear strike, three at a time would work 12-hour shifts. Whoever was on shift at the time of a strike had to remain for up to three weeks, monitoring fallout levels.

A pinhole camera above ground would record the detonation, whether in the air or at ground level, and a series of these images could be used to determine exactly where the detonation took place and how powerful it was. This bunker was one of a series within sight of Birmingham, which was a likely target, but far enough away to be on the periphery of expected damage.

Although protected in a concrete bunker, the volunteers had no air filtration and no Personal Protective Equipment, aside from a dosimeter that measured accumulated radioactivity exposure. Time was spent above ground collecting wind speed, wind direction and radiation measurements, and conducting maintenance tasks. When one person's dose reached a limit, someone else would perform those functions instead.

Fortunately, this system was never tested, although the bunker remained in use until 1991, by which time hostilities were deemed to have diminished. In the light of an increasingly hostile Russian state, the UK's 2025 Strategic Defence Review committed to a significant modernisation of its nuclear deterrent. Let's hope bunkers like this will never need to be put back into service.

ADDRESS Middle Hill, Broadway, WR12 7LB (park at Broadway Tower and head to the northernmost part of the car park), www.broadwaytower.co.uk/nuclear-bunker
TIP There is a café at Broadway Tower, and for a wider range of refreshment options, head straight down the footpath from the tower into the village.

12 National Collection of Telephone Kiosks

Changing communication

Scouts have long had the motto 'Be prepared'. In the early 1980s, one of the ways in which they were often encouraged to be prepared was to always have a 10p piece in their pocket. For those born in the 21st century, that might seem a little odd, but at the time, it made perfect sense because this was how much it cost to make a local call from a public phone box.

When telephony was first introduced, only wealthy households had their own phones. A village might have another 'call office' that was controlled by an attendant – and only available when they were. As use of this new means of communication spread, this became a touch inconvenient, and, in 1922, the telephone kiosk with a pre-paid coin box was introduced. The iconic red phone box we all know and love was the K6 – the sixth standard design. It was introduced in 1935 to commemorate King George V's Silver Jubilee, and the General Post Office, the state monopoly responsible for the telephone system, pledged to site one in every village that also had a post office, regardless of whether it was commercially viable. Suddenly, most villages in the country had a bright red phone box, although in places of outstanding natural beauty, they were grey or cream with red window frames.

It is rare to find a phone in a telephone kiosk these days – they are more likely to house a defibrillator or village library. A 50p coin was minted to commemorate the Scouts' centenary in 2007, but the demise of the coin-operated phone box would have made that fairly useless for being prepared. Who would have thought that, these days, Scouts are more likely to 'Be prepared' by having their own phone fully charged in their pocket? For a taste of the past, Avoncroft Museum has recreated a fully functioning telephone exchange so we can all experience making a call the old-fashioned, and once 'newfangled', way.

ADDRESS Avoncroft Museum, Bromsgrove, B60 4JR, +44 (0) 1527 831363, www.avoncroft.org.uk **TIP** Although 11,000 K8-design telephone kiosks were installed from 1968–1984, not many have survived. There is a rare example on the westbound platform of Worcester Shrub Hill railway station.

13 Railway Workers' Graves

An unwelcome surprise

On Tuesday, 10 November 1840, John Rutherford, Thomas Scaife and colleagues headed into work for the Birmingham and Gloucester Railway Company, as usual. Maybe they hadn't slept well, for they all knew a big day was ahead. Maybe they were excited about being the first to test a new steam engine. Or maybe they were fearful or had a sense of foreboding about what was to come. We will never know. What we do know is that neither of these men returned home alive after work that day.

The locomotive *Surprise* had been adapted to improve performance. Trains faced a particular challenge when heading from Bromsgrove into Birmingham, up 2.5 miles of the Lickey Incline, so this was the perfect place to test it. The company's engineer and foreman both examined the engine and were happy to take it out for a run. It was placed on the line and brought up to steam. After several short runs, in which nothing untoward happened, the engine was stationary at Bromsgrove station. Coal was added to the boiler to bring it back up to steam, and, living up to the locomotive's name, it exploded. Thomas Scaife, the 28-year-old driver, died on the spot. John Rutherford, the 32-year-old foreman, died 12 hours later in hospital. Several others were injured.

A report was made and an inquest held, at which the two deceased were exonerated from blame. After a short adjournment, the boiler manufacturer was questioned, and the jury concluded that the incident was caused by the use of substandard materials.

That was probably of little consolation to John Rutherford's widow, who erected this gravestone in his honour. The men's colleagues clubbed together for a similar memorial for Thomas Scaife. The unusual nature of these gravestones and the story they tell has encouraged local people to cherish them, repairing and refurbishing them as required to keep their memories alive.

ADDRESS St John's Churchyard (44 yards north of the church), Kidderminster Road, Bromsgrove, B61 7JW **TIP** The Bromsgrove Society has created two walks around the cemetery, which lies to the north of the graveyard (www.bsoc.co.uk/cemetery-walk).

14 Wyre Forest

England's largest woodland
National Nature Reserve

If you don't like trees, then Wyre Forest is probably not the place for you; here, the trees are the stars of the show. This is the remains of an ancient coppiced oak woodland, some of which is still being managed that way – cutting down most of the trees over a 15 to 20 year cycle to produce long, straight stems for uses like basket making, firewood and charcoal, while leaving some to grow tall and straight to be cut for uses like construction. These oaks have been supplemented with conifers to help meet the demand for fast-growing softwoods, creating a mosaic of woodland habitats.

Trees might be centre stage here, but they have a fabulous supporting cast. Coppicing allows light to reach the woodland floor, creating ideal conditions for ground flora such as bluebells and wild garlic in spring. Listen out for the drumming of woodpeckers and look out for their loping flight pattern between the trees. All three native species live here: Lesser Spotted, Greater Spotted and Green Woodpeckers. The forest also supports 33 species of butterfly, including the White Admiral, and over 1,000 species of moth.

Mammals that call the forest home include polecats, otters, dormice and rats, as well as fallow deer, whose rather enthusiastic rutting (mating) can be dangerous for humans who get too close. Some paths are closed during autumn for safety reasons, but you might still hear the distinctive throaty belching noises the bucks make, which are, apparently, attractive to the does.

And not only is the forest attractive to wildlife, it is also set up to make access for humans easy. A large parking area has toilet facilities, a visitor centre and café, and an all-terrain electric scooter hire shop, if you are reliant on wheels. There are trails throughout the forest, and even a high-ropes course for those who would like to see it from a different angle.

ADDRESS Callow Hill, DY14 9XQ, www.forestryengland.uk/wyre-forest
TIP If you fancy a pub meal after your visit to the forest, the Royal Forester Country Inn in Callow Hill is popular with diners (www.royalforesterinn.co.uk).

15 Point-to-Point Racing

Can you see the church yet?

Point-to-point racing started over 200 years ago, when landowners or members of hunts started to race each other from one point to another across the countryside, jumping any obstacles such as fences or streams they encountered along the way. Over time, the participants started to use village churches as the finish line, because their steeples were visible from afar. This explains why horse racing over fences and ditches is known as *steeplechasing*. These days, point-to-point racing is usually conducted around a circuit rather than across open country. Most races are three miles long over 18 fences.

Second only to football, horse racing is one of the largest spectator sports in Britain. However, only a small proportion of jockeys start their career on the professional circuit. The sport offers a route into professional racing, beginning with pony racing for the youngest riders. Once they reach the age of 16, jockeys keen for a professional career usually turn to pointing, where they can gain experience and develop racing skills in a more relaxed environment than professional events.

The relaxed environment extends to the spectators. At Chaddesley Corbett, you will find the usual trappings of a racecourse: food vendors, bars and bookies. You will also find generations of families converging for a picnic on the grass overlooking the track for a fun day out. Here, you can get close enough to the horses to feel their energy and the trembling of the earth as they thunder past. The events are fiercely competitive, belying the riders' amateur status. This is where you will see the stars of the future cutting their teeth and fighting for their place in the professional horse racing world. Chaddesley Corbett Racecourse offers four fixtures between December and May, so check out the website, dig out some warm clothes, and prepare for a fabulous day out.

ADDRESS Kidderminster Road, Chaddesley Corbett, DY10 4QT, www.chaddesleyraces.co.uk **TIP** If you'd like to see some professional horse racing, then head over to Worcester Racecourse (www.worcester-racecourse.co.uk).

16 The Lenches Amphitheatre

The show must go on!

Given Britain's unpredictable weather, a love of outdoor theatre is somewhat unlikely. However, it is something people in Britain seem to have embraced, at least since the Romans arrived and started to build amphitheatres for their own special brand of entertainment. In those days, the 'entertainment' often revolved around cruelty and loss of life, to both animals and people, with the audience baying for blood. These days, outdoor theatre in Britain does not harm animals, and actors are generally safe from one another, although they might receive a drenching if the weather is inclement. And, of course, the audiences are generally more reserved – until it comes to applause, that is.

British people love to celebrate the summer by watching outdoor theatre and films, even if it entails wrapping themselves in blankets, wearing winter bobble hats, sheltering under umbrellas, and drinking flasks of tea in a bid to stay warm. The Lenches have fully embraced this tradition in the 21st century. The sports and recreation club saw an opportunity in a curve of land above its sports pitch, with distant views to the west over the Malvern and Clent Hills. With the help of the local council, businesses and community, it carved amphitheatre seating into that enticing slope. This is not your run-of-the-mill semi-circular amphitheatre, but curvaceous terraces following the line of the land, overlooking an equally curvaceous stage.

Several plays are performed here during the summer season, and occasionally a film is shown, all vying with the view for attention. Each terrace is wide enough to fit a camping chair, so – in good weather at least – the audience can make themselves comfortable. And if liquid sunshine is the order of the day? Well, then, there are always umbrellas, blankets, woolly hats and flasks of tea to fall back on, in true British style. The show must go on!

ADDRESS Ab Lench Road, Church Lench, WR11 4UQ, www.lenchestheatre.co.uk
TIP The Lenches Club, next door to the amphitheatre, welcomes visitors as well as members (www.thelenches.org.uk/the-lenches-club).

17 Churchill Forge

A wheely interesting day out

Water powered many industries in Britain until the advent of the steam engine. At the time the Domesday Book was written at the end of the 11th century, there were 6,000 mills in England, and that number rose over the following centuries. Even when larger industrial sites had switched to steam engines in the 18th and 19th centuries, small rural mills remained in operation. This is one example, where tools such as ladles for the Stourbridge glass industry, specialist shovels for the Droitwich Spa salt industry (known as skippets), and spades and other garden tools were made.

The water wheels here were overshot, meaning water was fed into buckets near the top, and its weight turned the wheel. These wheels are both 17 feet in diameter and turn in opposite directions, so the drive shaft from one leads into the southern mill and the other leads into the northern mill. The northern mill building housed a drop hammer, pneumatic hammers and a press, and the southern mill building powered the furnace blower. Although this is a peaceful agricultural area now, this was one of ten water mills within a mile of this site – it was once a busy industrial zone, supplying materials to the larger factories of the West Midlands.

Despite the introduction of steam power, some water mills continued to operate well into the 20th century. In fact, it seems a little incongruous to realise that this mill was in operation until the year in which people first walked on the moon. Since it was closed in 1969, the descendants of the final miller have looked after the site, now as trustees of the mill's preservation charity. The mill holds monthly open days in the summer, at which time, the wheels and machinery are brought back into operation to demonstrate what was once a commercial operation on this site. It will also open for educational and other groups.

ADDRESS Churchill Lane, Churchill, DY10 3LX, www.churchillforge.org.uk
TIP An altogether different type of pressing is done at a cider mill. To see the most modern equipment in use, take a tour at Oldfields Cider in the Teme Valley (www.oldfieldscider.co.uk).

18 Four Stones

A picturesque picnic site

In Worcestershire, there are no prehistoric standing stones or stone circles. So, why can a group of standing stones be found here on the top of the Clent Hills? The answer lies in the Industrial Revolution. During this period, practicality often overshadowed beauty, and ugly urban areas were growing. In response to this, the landed gentry began looking towards beauty and sublimity and creating a form of romantic escapism on their land. Around their new houses, they created picturesque gardens that extended into the surrounding landscape, reflecting a reverence for nature and an idealisation of the past.

This led to the construction of many follies, including buildings such as Broadway Tower, which were designed to resemble medieval castles. Lord Lyttleton of Hagley Hall was particularly prolific and inventive in his construction of follies, and it was he who chose to create a megalithic monument on the summit of the Clent Hills in the late 18th century.

Prehistoric standing stones were often raised singly or arranged in a circle. In Scotland and north-east England, some are arranged to create a square or rectangle. These are known as four-posters. The layout of the Four Stones does not match any of these ancient ideas. It seems more likely that they were arranged to create a dramatic silhouette on the hilltop and to frame the views from this point. Reaching the stones would also have offered a reward to those who expended the effort to climb to the top of the hill, just as they do today.

These days, the Clent Hills are not part of an estate that is purely there for the enjoyment of the aristocracy. Instead, they are owned by the National Trust and managed for public access as well as nature and landscape conservation. This makes the Four Stones a popular place to visit with a picnic on a summer's day, and with a west-facing view, it is also an ideal place to enjoy the sunset.

ADDRESS A half-hour walk uphill from the car park on Adam's Hill, DY9 9PS
TIP Hagley Park, in which more of Lord Lyttleton's follies can be seen, is a five-minute drive to the north (www.hagleypark.co.uk).

19 Defford Radio Telescope

A magic eye that's out of this world

When we look up into the night sky, even with the most powerful visible light telescope, we can only see a tiny fraction of what is out there. The Hubble Space Telescope helps by providing a viewpoint that is not pegged to Earth. However, that still cannot see everything that is happening. If we expand our range of 'vision' to include radio waves, we can learn a lot more.

Defford Radio Telescope, which is best seen from the road north of Defford, is one of seven across the UK that combine to form the national radio telescope, known as e-MERLIN. A superfast optical fibre network links all the individual telescopes to Jodrell Bank, where the signals are converted into data, which can then be transformed into images within our visual range. The telescopes can pick up radio waves emitted by things as small as a molecule or as large as a galaxy, helping scientists better understand the extraterrestrial world. The images can be overlaid on visual-light images from telescopes such as the Hubble Space Telescope or even used in the Search for Extraterrestrial Intelligence (SETI).

e-MERLIN is the only radio telescope in the world that has enough resolution to study the formation of planets. Since its inception, it has been used to discover around 2,000 of them, along with discs of gas and dust that are thought to be the early stages of planet formation. Things are expected to change in the early 2030s, when South Africa's Square Kilometre Array (SKA) will join the race and provide even more detailed images.

Next time you look up into the night sky and see apparently static stars and planets with nothing in between, perhaps it will be a good time to consider everything that is happening just outside your field of vision, and how we are continuing to develop magic eyes that can increasingly understand what else is going on that is out of this world.

ADDRESS Defford Airfield, WR8 9DW **TIP** RAF Defford Museum at National Trust Croome is a great place to learn more about the airbase's role in developing RADAR, which was crucial to the Allies' victory in World War II (www.nationaltrust.org.uk).

20 Church of the Sacred Heart

Magnificent mosaics

From the outside, the Church of the Sacred Heart in Droitwich Spa is a little surprising, as it was built to the design of a Roman basilica. A square campanile stands to one side of the main building, linked by a single storey. The ensemble looks as if it belongs in an Italian city.

However, the surprising architecture does not at all prepare unsuspecting visitors for the astonishing interior décor. The door leads into a dim entry hall, with leaflets and an electronic donation point. So far, so normal. Look up, and a pair of mosaic peacocks stand on either side of an arch. These are beautiful and deserve some attention before you enter the main body of the church.

Light shoots across the space, the mosaics giving you the effect of being in a giant, golden (cuboid!) glitterball. The impact is electric. Once over the initial shock of sensory overwhelm, more attention can be paid to the details. Walking towards the altar, you face Jesus with arms outstretched. To the right are panels depicting St Richard de Wyche, the local patron saint, and to the left, others depicting scenes from the Bible. Every surface above shoulder height is carpeted in Venetian glass tiles, either coloured or sandwiching real gold leaf. Restoration in 2025 has left the church glowing, and whether by accident or design, the mosaicist has placed some of the candle tiles at just the right angle to catch the light from the windows. There are stories and symbolism everywhere, from an owl positioned to help keep the congregation awake during sermons to a carving of a person holding a finger to their lips, encouraging seemly behaviour.

Once you think you have seen everything and turn to leave, the most impressive mural of all comes into view – that of the Holy Trinity, surrounded by the Nine Choirs of Angels and the three Archangels – one final feast for your eyes.

ADDRESS 208 Worcester Road, Droitwich Spa, WR9 8AZ, +44 (0) 1905 773258, www.sacredheartdroitwich.org.uk **TIP** Mosaics are not found only in churches. Head to Milward Square in the Kingfisher Centre in Redditch and look up to see some designed by Eduardo Paolozzi, whose work can also be seen in Tottenham Court Road underground station in London (www.kingfishershopping.co.uk).

21 *Salt Worker*

An evaporating enterprise

Two hundred million years ago, the land beneath Droitwich Spa was part of Pangaea, a supercontinent larger than all of today's continents combined. The world was considerably warmer, and the land was closer to the equator, making it far hotter than it is now. From time to time, the area was flooded with seawater. The heat caused the water to evaporate, leaving salt deposits that thickened after each flooding event. Later, the salt was covered by sediment, and under the pressure of gravity and the sediment above, the two layers consolidated into rock salt and clay.

The tectonic plates slowly moved north to their current position and tilted. Water infiltrated the rock salt and was forced through cracks in the clay to create briny springs in the Droitwich Spa area. Since the Iron Age, the brine has been collected, re-evaporated, and the resulting salt traded. In the Victorian era, a canal was built to transport salt to the River Severn at Gloucester, where large docks provided infrastructure for onward distribution.

Droitwich Spa prospered thanks to this industry. However, in the early 20th century the industry faltered. The saltworks fell into disrepair, and the workers' accommodation became slums. Both were demolished, and Vines Park, where the *Salt Worker* sculpture stands, was created in 1935 on the site of those buildings.

Almost a century later, salt production restarted on a local farm, the canal was reinstated, and this sculpture was erected to commemorate all the people who once worked in the industry that shaped this town. The sculpture is made from almost 3,000 metal plates designed to resemble salt crystals, and it stands on the outline of the *Volunteer*, one of the barges that once transported these valuable crystals to Gloucester. It was made by Pershore blacksmith Steve Ellis Cooper and is based on a 2015 tree carving by Tom Harvey.

ADDRESS Vines Park, Kidderminster Road, Droitwich Spa, WR9 8LB
TIP Droitwich Spa celebrates its association with salt production at its annual summer Saltfest, which offers music, food, crafting, theatre, comedy and fireworks (www.saltfestdroitwich.co.uk).

22 St Peter's Fields

These trees are no joke

Douglas, towering over Scot, bragged he was the star of the arboretum. His friend replied, 'Fine – but I'm the one visitors pine for after they've been for a swim in the lido'.

Douglas firs can reach over 200 feet in height, well above Britain's native Scots pine at a mere 115 feet. Even so, unless you see two trees of the same age standing next to each other, how could you tell the difference? First, there's the bark; on a Scots pine, it's brown and flaky with an orange hue, and on a Douglas fir, it's purplish-brown, with horizontal cracks appearing as it ages. The needles are also very different – those of a Douglas fir, at around half an inch long, are less than half the size of a Scots pine's. Looking at the needles of a conifer is a good way to distinguish between fir, spruce and pine species generally. Fir needles are soft and flat and grow from a single point. Spruce needles are short, stiff and rounded. And pine needles are often soft and long, growing in clusters.

Fir, spruce and pine all grow in St Peter's Fields, along with other trees, with paths winding between them. This green lung in the heart of Droitwich Spa was created because a far-sighted GP in the 1950s could see the town expanding and understood the health benefits of green space. The council paid only 10 shillings for the farmland, which it has now turned into an arboretum that borders the park next to the lido, offering walking and running trails right in the heart of the town. A small stream runs through the arboretum, and the boardwalk through the willow carr (wet woodland) offers a change of scene.

As most conifers are evergreen, growing and dropping needles throughout the seasons, the arboretum maintains its form all year. When winter settled over the arboretum, Douglas boasted he still looked magnificent. Scot just smiled. 'We're evergreens,' he said. 'We don't have an off-season.'

ADDRESS The Holloway, Droitwich Spa, WR9 7AT, www.wychavon.gov.uk/park-and-open-spaces **TIP** Droitwich Spa Lido, with its heated, saline pool, is next to the arboretum (www.riversfitness.co.uk/droitwichlido).

23 Alabaster Statues

A glowing tribute

Alabaster is a soft, opaque, and usually pale stone that was popular for church carvings throughout the medieval period. Unfortunately, most of this statuary was destroyed during Henry VIII's Reformation in the 16th century, when he split from the Church of Rome and created the Church of England. After this time, the stone remained popular for funerary carvings because its crystalline structure makes it translucent when thin enough, so the edges of statues appear to glow when lit from behind. Most were probably carved in Nottingham, which specialised as the country's centre of funerary alabaster carving.

When this memorial was crafted in the 17th century, the Savages were Lords of the Manor in Elmley Castle (the lowest class of the aristocracy, below Barons, Earls, Dukes and the King).

This tomb commemorates the lives of three members of the family: the father, his son, and his wife. Catherine is holding an infant, indicating that one of her children predeceased her. The four characters kneeling at the end of the monument represent the four children who lived. To a modern audience, this might be the end of it, but to an illiterate member of the congregation in the 17th century, this tomb would have told a story. The children's pose indicates piety, and their presence on the tomb would tell everyone that there were descendants to continue the family line.

Catherine has a unicorn's head at her feet, symbolising chastity, fidelity and moral purity – all the virtues expected of a woman of her status at the time. The lions' heads at the feet of the men symbolise strength and nobility. And these two animals, combining the royal emblems of Scotland and England, also symbolise allegiance to the crown, realigning the Savages with the Royal Family shortly after the restoration of the monarchy that followed the British Civil Wars.

ADDRESS St Mary's Church, Elmley Castle, WR10 3HT TIP Impressive alabaster funerary statues can also be seen at the Church of St Mary Magdalene in Croome D'Abitot, WR8 9DW.

24 Parsons' Folly

The world's least picturesque 'picturesque' folly?

Parsons' Folly is thought to have been built by local landowning gentleman John Parsons during a period when building follies to make the landscape more 'picturesque' was the height of fashion. Adding a prominent tower, perhaps used as a summerhouse, to an existing ancient landscape such as this Iron Age hill fort would have conveyed status to all who could see it.

The tower is 39 feet tall, on a summit that rises to 961 feet above sea level. Local rumour has it that the tower was built to turn the hill into a mountain, as the combined height above sea level is exactly 1,000 feet. Could this possibly be true? First, there is the question of what constitutes a mountain. Everyone knows a mountain is bigger than a hill, but how much bigger? And is it the overall height above sea level that counts, or the height above the surrounding land? Astonishingly, there is no widely accepted answer to these questions, and 1,000 feet is certainly not a magical hill-to-mountain number, despite that being the premise of the 1995s film *The Englishman Who Went Up a Hill But Came Down a Mountain*.

Next is the question of measurement. The Ordnance Survey first published maps of the UK in the 19th century, after it is thought this tower was built. With no map, it was unlikely that John Parsons would have known how high the hill was. So, it seems more likely that the combined height of hill and tower is a coincidence, and that he simply wanted to make his land seem more impressive than it was and offer evidence of his status, with no real consideration of overall height.

From a distance, Parsons' Tower does look impressive; a little like the tower of a long-ruined castle. But up close? No castellations. No gothic flourishes. Just a plain, square tower, now bristling with communications equipment. Could it possibly be the least picturesque 'picturesque' folly in the world?

ADDRESS Elmley Castle, WR10 3DN. Accessible by footpath from the top of Hill Lane. TIP Take a close look at Banbury Stone, a few yards to the north of the tower, and you might see the shape of an elephant.

25 Sundial in the Churchyard

An arc of accuracy

Sundials can be found on stone walls all across Worcestershire. This is a particularly fine example of several dial types and styles, dating from the 17th century. Reading a sundial is, of course, simple, but the mathematics behind them is rather more complicated.

If you were to stand a vertical post in the ice at the North or South Pole, its shadow would move by 15 degrees every hour as the Earth spins. So, a horizontal sundial at either pole would have evenly spaced lines marking the hours. Elsewhere, calculations are required to account for latitude and longitude, compass bearing and angle of the surfaces used. Even for a perfectly adjusted sundial, the sun's angle varies in three-month cycles, so determining the exact time requires additional calculations. And that is before consideration is given to daylight saving in the summer months.

Ultimately, sundials were never designed to tell the time that accurately. They did not need to be used to coordinate activities across distance, but provided a local guide during a period when knowing the hour was enough for most people, most of the time. The time across the UK was not standardised into a single time zone until the advent of train travel, when it became inconvenient to keep adjusting clocks and timetables.

Since then, timekeeping accuracy has undergone several iterations. Pendulum clocks and spring watches were considered accurate enough until quartz clocks were invented, relying on the consistent vibration of quartz crystals to keep time. Atomic clocks are even more accurate, and used by modern technology, with their accuracy measured in seconds per billions of years. More technologies are on the horizon, but there is something soothing about a clock that simply moves round in time with the sun arcing across the sky. After all, isn't that enough accuracy for most of us, most of the time?

ADDRESS St Mary's Church, Elmley Castle, WR10 3HT **TIP** If you look up at the corner of Foregate Street and Sansome Street in Worcester, you will see what looks like a double clock. The lower face tells the time, the upper indicates the weather conditions.

26 Bell Tower

Saved by the bell

Evesham was always a pious place. It was founded in a loop of the River Avon where, at the beginning of the 8th century, a swineherd called Eof saw a vision of the Virgin Mary. Word of this reached the Bishop of Worcester, who visited the area and had the same vision himself. Seeing this as a sign from God, the bishop founded a monastery there and called the area Eof's Homme – Eof's Land – which eventually became Evesham.

For 800 years, the abbey thrived. In the 11th century, the Normans invaded, and the abbey continued unhindered. In the 12th century, King Henry II visited – at least three times. In the 13th century, Simon de Montfort, the Earl of Leicester, challenged the power of the throne, an action that first led to a civil war and then to the beginnings of democracy in Britain. He died while battling Prince Edward's army in Evesham and was buried at the abbey. Throughout this period, the monks made wine, distributed alms to the poor, educated boys, produced manuscripts and literary works, and managed their estates and churches from the abbey. The market town of Evesham expanded to serve all this activity.

In the 16th century, the abbey met its demise when King Henry VIII dissolved the monasteries. The buildings were quickly demolished, and most of the land was granted to Sir Philip Hobby. The exception was the bell tower, which remained too valuable to give away, as it had lead on the roof and at least one bell still hanging. Luckily for us, these were not sold during Henry's lifetime, so the tower remained. Queen Mary I, whose reign followed, was a devoted Catholic and did not want to see the tower destroyed. Consequently, she donated the tower and the remaining bell to the town of Evesham, thereby saving this campanile from the fate of the rest of the abbey. It seems it is not only boxers who are saved by the bell!

ADDRESS Abbey Road, Evesham, WR11 4RW, www.eveshamabbey.org.uk TIP Illuminated manuscripts from Evesham Abbey and other monastic centres can be viewed by appointment at Worcester Cathedral Library (www.worcestercathedral.org.uk/heritage/library).

27 Hampton Ferry

Making a habit of wine

The Benedictine monks at Evesham Abbey lived by a complex series of rules established by St Benedict himself, as do those in Benedictine communities today. The rule about drinking wine is straightforward: it is best to abstain. However, St Benedict recognised that everyone has their gifts, and strength in this matter might not be one of them. Therefore, his rule permits monks to drink one hemina of wine a day (roughly one large glass in today's measures) and no more. Exceptions exist if they are doing hard manual labour or it is particularly hot, but under no circumstances must drunkenness be permitted.

This rule does not mean that monks can expect a glass of wine a day; it explicitly states that monks must not complain if circumstances are such that wine is not available to them. For those who enjoy a tipple, it is therefore wise to ensure they always have some to hand, and one way to do this is to make their own. This is exactly what the monks of Evesham Abbey did. The land in the loop of the river in which the abbey was built was probably a bit too wet for vines to thrive, and having higher land all around could create a frost pocket, so they planted their vineyard on the far side of the river, to the west of the town, on a slope. This meant the monks needed a way to cross the river to tend the vines, so the Hampton Ferry was established.

It is thought to have been operating for almost 800 years, although if you use it, you might be glad to know that the boat itself has been replaced to ensure river-worthiness! Unfortunately, there is no longer a vineyard on the far side of the river. Instead, the ferry provides transport for villagers and visitors staying in the caravan park to the town side of the river and back again. As a result, it only operates in the summer months – it's wise to check the website for sailing times.

ADDRESS Boat Lane, Evesham, WR11 4BP, www.hamptonferry.co.uk **TIP** Cross on the ferry and head uphill, then turn right onto Red Lane past the comms tower to visit the Woodland Trust's Eoves Wood. Planted for the millennium, it has views over Evesham and to Bredon Hill (www.woodlandtrust.org.uk).

28 The Wood Norton

A place of exile

The French Revolution at the end of the 18th century abolished feudalism. A few years later, the nobility was restored, albeit without privileges. This system continued until 1870, when nobles lost their legal status, although they were permitted to use their titles as part of their names. Following this change, an exiled French duke bought the Wood Norton estate as hunting grounds. When he died, the estate passed to his great-nephew, the Duke of Orléans, a pretender to the French throne. It was this duke who built the hall we now see, including the rather austere marble bathroom with the French fleur-de-lys mosaic on the floor, which was retained in subsequent refurbishments. The duke and several of his family members lived here and used it as a royal palace. Living in exile themselves, it is perhaps no surprise that they offered a temporary home to King Manuel and Queen Amélie of Portugal when they were deposed and exiled in 1910.

The next exiles to be housed at Wood Norton were working for the BBC during World War II. The corporation had bought the site before the war started in case it needed to relocate away from London. Temporary buildings were constructed in the grounds, and by 1940, 1,300 programmes were being broadcast from the site every week, making it one of the largest broadcasting centres in Europe. For four years, the site also served as a monitoring centre, housing people from other European countries to translate intercepted messages. At one point, over 1,000 people worked on the site, all billeted in Evesham. The locals had to accept them, even though they were given no clue as to why they were there. During the 1960s, a new wing was added to the hall, with a large nuclear bunker underneath, which has luckily never been needed.

Happily, Wood Norton is now a hotel and restaurant, so you don't need to be in exile to enjoy the facilities.

ADDRESS Worcester Road, Evesham, WR11 4YB, www.thewoodnorton.com
TIP Secrecy still surrounds the nuclear bunker at the Wood Norton. In contrast, the one in Drakelow Tunnels near Kidderminster is open once or twice a month for guided tours (www.drakelowtunnels.co.uk).

29 Simply Alpaca

The county's cutest lawn mowers

In Andean mythology, alpacas were a precious gift from the goddess Pachamama, and they will remain on Earth only as long as they are respected and cared for. Indigenous people kept them as livestock on the Altiplano – the high plateau in central South America – for their fleeces. When the Spanish conquistadors arrived, many alpacas were replaced by sheep, and it was left to subsistence farmers to continue with the tradition.

Fast-forward 300 years, and Sir Titus Salt, the Victorian industrialist who set up the model town of Saltaire in Yorkshire, found some unwanted bales of alpaca fleece in a warehouse. Curious, he spent the next 18 months devising a process that turned them into a durable, luxurious cloth, loved by wealthy Victorians. Garments made from alpaca were so valuable and long-lived that they were bequeathed to future generations.

Around the turn of the current millennium, alpacas started to be imported to the UK, where they have adapted well to our climate. They have experienced a surge in popularity since then and can often be seen on country walks in Worcestershire. Many are kept as pets, providing a cute addition to the garden as well as lawn-mowing services. Much of their popularity stems from their curious, gentle nature, which is why they are also popular with petting farms. Spend some time with alpacas, and you start to feel their aura of calm wash over you. Here at Simply Alpaca, you can visit with the herd or take a walk with them in the surrounding countryside. Alternatively, you can arrange for them to be transported to you for a special event. The animals are also used for therapy because they are so relaxed.

For those who enjoy crafting, there are workshops where you can create beautiful fabrics or yarns of your own, and a shop where you can acquire supplies or beautiful items ready made.

ADDRESS Kings Lodge, Alcester Road, Flyford Flavell, WR7 4DF, +44 (0) 7980 587562, www.simplyalpaca.co.uk TIP For a tasty breakfast or lunch, head to Toast on the main road in Flyford Flavell. In winter, they have a roaring log fire, and in summer, plenty of outdoor space (www.uktoast.co.uk).

30 Grafton Wood

Home to Brown Hairstreak butterflies

Populations of Brown Hairstreak butterflies have declined significantly over the last 50 years. They are found mainly in the south of the country, and this is one of the most northerly places you can see them, although they remain elusive.

Your best bet is to take a walk in Grafton Wood in August or September. Look up at the ash trees along the rides or the woodland boundary. If you see a cluster of butterflies, it could be Brown Hairstreaks, congregating to mate and feeding on aphid honeydew. The females will drop down to near eye height when they are ready to lay their eggs, so look out for a brown butterfly with orange splodges on its forewings and darker orange tails on its hindwings, flying along the scrub layer edging the paths. If you see one at rest, it is likely to have its wings closed. The underwings are coppery with two wavy white streaks. However, you are more likely to see their eggs, laid in the junction of twigs on young blackthorns. Looking like tiny white sea urchins, they contrast well with the dark bark.

These butterflies have seen such a significant decline because they lay their eggs almost exclusively on blackthorn bushes. These bushes, the first to flower in spring, are mainly found in hedgerows, and many hedgerows have been removed to make bigger fields. Others are often flailed every year, which destroys the eggs. That makes reserves like this crucial to the survival of the species, and the management work that has been done here – creating rides, planting new blackthorn bushes and cutting back old ones so they will produce new growth – has resulted in an increase in the number and range of Brown Hairstreaks in this area.

Park in the church car park (it's private – please be considerate and leave a donation in the honesty box). Walk out of the far end and turn right. Follow the yellow public footpath signs to the wood.

ADDRESS Grafton Flyford, WR7 4PG, www.worcswildlifetrust.co.uk
TIP Only a few miles away, Trench Wood Nature Reserve is another place you might spot Brown Hairstreak butterflies. It is also managed to provide an ideal habitat for warblers (www.worcswildlifetrust.co.uk).

31 Finest Baroque Church

Reuse, restore, regild

In a slightly different take on the usual concept of 'reduce, reuse, recycle', much of the decoration in Great Witley Parish Church was not new when it was installed. When the church was consecrated in 1735, it was plainly decorated. It was not until the later part of the century that it gained its Baroque style, when the owner of Cannon's Palace near London needed to sell much of his estate. The second Lord Foley, who owned the church and Witley Court, bought most of the chapel's interior decoration and transported it here.

The paintings were relatively easy to move, as they were nailed to a wooden frame, rather than painted onto plaster. It must have taken more care and skill to successfully transport the stained-glass and enamel-painted windows from London to Worcestershire on roads as poor as they were then. Luckily, there was no need to try to move the plasterwork. Instead, moulds of it were taken, and a papier-mâché replica was recreated to fit the church here at Great Witley. The gold leaf was new. It is almost pure gold, mixed with a tiny amount of other metals to improve its longevity.

In the 1800s, the church gained some more new decoration. The black-and-white marble floor, new pews, a font and a pulpit were added. It was also refaced on the outside to match the recently refurbished Witley Court. In the 1910s, the panels were added behind the altar. These are made with real gold leaf between layered glass and were made in Venice.

In 1937, the house suffered from an enormous fire, and both the house and the church were left to deteriorate. However, in the 1960s, the parishioners took it upon themselves to lead a restoration project. Since then, much work has been done in an ongoing programme to restore and regild what has become Britain's finest Baroque church, ensuring its preservation for future generations.

ADDRESS St Michael and All Angels, Great Witley, WR6 6JT, www.greatwitleychurch.org.uk **TIP** English Heritage maintains the ruins of Witley Court next to the church. It's the perfect place to go for a picnic while watching the spectacular fountains or enjoying lunch at the café (www.english-heritage.org.uk).

32 The Falconry Centre

Captivity and conservation

Have you ever looked into the eyes of an owl? You are unlikely to be able to do so very often in the wild. After all, owls are usually well camouflaged, tend to be shy of humans and are often nocturnal – but not always. Did you know that if you do get close enough to see the colour of their eyes, you can tell what time of day they prefer to hunt? Yellow-eyed owls, with eyes the colour of the sun, tend to prefer to hunt during the day. You might see a Little Owl perching during daylight hours, peering out at you with its yellow eyes, but only if you are observant – their camouflage is pretty good! In contrast, owls like Barn Owls, with eyes the colour of the night sky, tend to prefer hunting at night, although we are most likely to see them at dawn and dusk.

At the Falconry Centre, owls are bred in two different ways. Some are kept with their parents, from whom they learn how to communicate and interact with other owls. Because owls are generally solitary, once mature, these individuals remain on their own until they are ready to breed. Other owls are introduced to a person or people when they are young. They are fed by hand, not by beak, and imprint on their human carers. These owls do not develop a fear of humans and can be introduced to new experiences, which means they often become ambassador owls, visiting schools and flying in demonstrations. Once you have looked into the eyes of an owl, you may never feel the same again!

As well as educating people about birds of prey, the Falconry Centre is part of a captive breeding programme for the Lugger Falcon. In the last 50 to 60 years, the population of this bird – native to the Indian subcontinent – has declined precipitously. Project Lugger aims to establish a healthy captive population, with the goal of releasing birds in areas where assisted recovery is most likely to succeed.

ADDRESS Kidderminster Road South, Hagley, DY9 0JB, +44 (0) 1562 700014, www.thefalconrycentre.co.uk TIP If you prefer to watch birds in the wild, try heading to Longdon and Eldersfield Marshes, Worcestershire Wildlife Trust's biggest conservation project (www.worcswildlifetrust.co.uk/nature-reserves/hill-court-farm-blacklands).

33 Wychbury Obelisk

Whistling in the wind

Fashion has never been confined to clothing; it can be seen in many different aspects of life, including landscape design. In the 18th century, a craze of building obelisks swept through the landowning classes, and this is one of them. Or should that be *was*? By the turn of this century, the Wychbury Obelisk was at risk of collapse. To restore it, every stone was removed, inspected and either reused or replaced, effectively making this a modern reconstruction. As the restoration was completed, a gift to future generations was built into the top – a time capsule. It contains contributions from local schoolchildren, a silver plaque stamped with the 2010 hallmarks and a whistle.

Not just any whistle. This is a whistle that tells a story, one that was invented in Birmingham in 1884 by Joseph Hudson, inspired by an advert placed by the Metropolitan Police. The Industrial Revolution had made London's public spaces noisier, and the police needed a means of communicating with their colleagues that was louder, more attention grabbing and easier to carry than the traditional rattle. Joseph Hudson rose to the challenge – he found that by adding a pea to a traditional whistle, it became shriller and louder. The Metropolitan whistle was born. Referees started using something similar in 1884, as whistling proved more effective at gaining attention than waving a handkerchief at errant players. The Acme Thunderer was born. Although now replaced for the highest-flight matches, the Acme Thunderer, still made in Birmingham, has been used by referees at every level of football, including in the 1966 World Cup, to signify the moment that the match really was all over now.

Just in case whistles have fallen out of fashion by the time the obelisk is next refurbished, future generations will be able to experience this iconic sound for themselves when the restoration programme starts.

ADDRESS DY9 9JY. Park on School Lane, Hagley, then walk up Monument Lane. At the top of the lane, keep ahead uphill on a public footpath, and you will soon see the obelisk. TIP If you love the sound of a referee's whistle, check out the match programme at nearby Stourbridge FC (www.stourbridgefc.com).

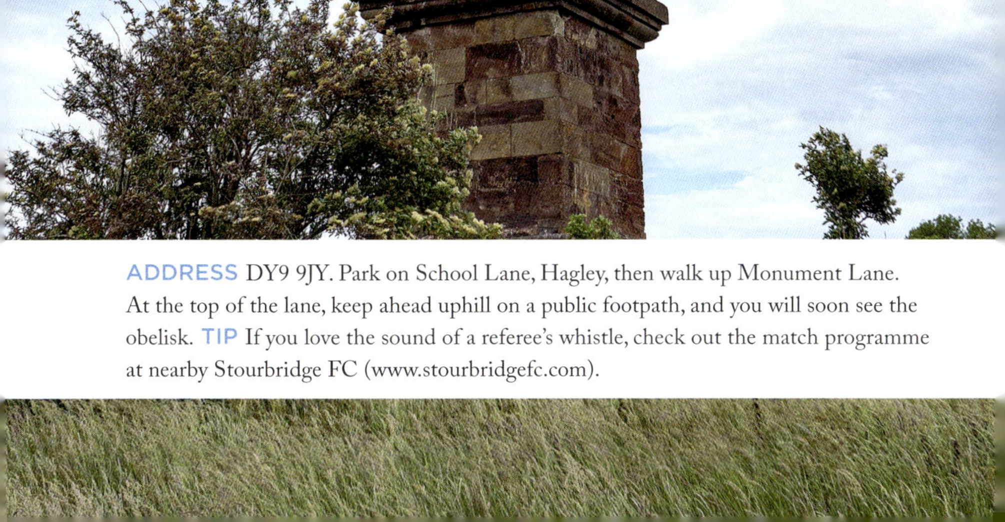

34 Three Kings Pub

No change here

If you are looking for a pub with a modern interior, great Wi-Fi, or even food, the Three Kings would not be a good choice. If you are looking for a pub on Tripadvisor, you will not find this one. If you are looking for a pub where the customer is always right, this might not be your best bet. And rumour has it, if you are looking for the Three Kings of nativity fame, you will not find them here; for this pub is, allegedly, named after the previous owners – the Kings. But that is way before living memory, as one other thing that has not changed here in a while is the ownership. The current licensee was born here, and the building has purportedly been in her family for over 300 years, although it wasn't a pub for the entire period.

It seems unlikely that the Three Kings' regulars want it to change. They probably don't want it to appear on Tripadvisor, either. They are happy to head over there for a good pint and a chat with people they know, and those who have found it by word of mouth. There is occasionally a rush when the local running club or cyclists drop in, and every year the pub holds a beer festival in November with a mass of morris dancers, but you'll have to be in the know to find out when it's happening.

And the best way to get in the know is probably to drop by and ask about it. And sink a pint in front of one of the fires, wondering about how many cigarettes it took to get the ceiling quite that shade of nicotine. Or whether the owners of the castle ever dropped in, for this building has outlived its fortified neighbour. If the walls could talk, the Three Kings would have a lot of gossip to share, but something about it suggests that it wouldn't; that it would prefer to stand silently, providing safe harbour in a turbulent world, while the locals continue to go about their business and enjoy a pint or two, unhindered by unnecessary change.

ADDRESS Church End, Hanley Castle, WR8 0BL, +44 (0) 1684 592686 **TIP** If you are looking for a more modern pub that serves good food, The Swan Inn over the road from the duck pond at Hanley Swan, a five-minute drive to the west, might just fit the bill (www.thehanleyswaninn.com).

35 Hartlebury Castle

Glory to God and goodwill to all men

As the Bishops of Worcester's residence from the 9th century through until the 21st, it is no surprise to find that Hartlebury Castle has a chapel. In 1675, the height of the chapel's roof was raised, but it was several decades later when the decoration we see today was added, by Bishop Maddox.

The oak from which the wood panelling is constructed was cut to make the most of the medullary rays, which radiate from the centre of the trunk to the bark. These structures transport nutrients and water through the tree while it is alive and can appear to shine like silver ribbons in the light once the wood has been cut. Stained-glass windows traditionally depict stories from the Bible, and that is exactly what the window in the chapel did when it was added in the 18th century. However, bishops are not above self-glorification. In 1898, Bishop Perowne removed the original window and replaced it with one featuring himself alongside Bishop Latimer, who was burned at the stake by Mary I in the 16th century. The dainty fan-vaulted plaster ceiling has been constructed over a sturdy, unseen wooden framework, which is fortunate, as children who played here in the 1950s used to jump into it from above in games of hide-and-seek.

Hartlebury Castle, an ancient site with a rich history, was originally built to defend the ford over the River Severn from Welsh invasions. Over the centuries, it has served various roles: a stopping point during military campaigns against Wales in 1282 and 1284, when the bishop's army bolstered the king's forces; a Royalist garrison during the British Civil Wars; and a Voluntary Aid Detachment hospital in World War I. It also housed bishops and their families for many centuries, as its primary function. As you would expect with this kind of history, the castle is filled with countless stories just waiting to be shared.

ADDRESS Hartlebury, DY11 7XZ, www.hartleburycastle.com **TIP** Once an inland port, Stourport Basin, a couple of miles to the west, is now popular with tourists, with funfairs, green spaces, cafés and pubs around the water.

36 Harvington Hall

Illusion confusion

When Henry VIII split from the Roman Catholic Church, a period of religious instability began. In the 11 years following his death, there were three monarchs, and the country vacillated between Catholic and Protestant worship. Edward VI was Protestant, and was followed by Mary I, who was Catholic. During the five years of Mary's reign, Protestants were persecuted, and hundreds were burned at the stake. This caused many to both fear and hate the Roman Catholic Church.

The next monarch was the Protestant Elizabeth I. She established the Anglican church in 1559, and the Book of Common Prayer became the only legal form of worship. A system of penalties was put in place for non-conformance, including hefty fines for missing Sunday communion. In the 1570s, an exiled English Catholic foresaw the end of the 'Old Faith' in England, so he started training missionaries to return and keep Catholicism alive. These priests gathered in 'safe houses' before moving on, and Harvington Hall was one of those houses. If caught, the priests were likely to be executed, so elaborate hiding places were created for them to escape to in case the house was searched. Harvington Hall was completely reconfigured and given a new staircase to create hidden spaces and confuse priest hunters. As a result, it has more priest hides than any other house.

The architect of these changes was Nicholas Owen, who was ultimately caught, sent to the Tower of London and tortured to death. He has since been canonised and, thanks to the nature of his work, is considered to be the patron saint of illusionists and escapologists.

It seems likely that the Anglican authorities knew about the role of Harvington Hall, as the Bishop of Worcester's residence is only a few miles away, yet as far as we know, it was never searched. It's almost a shame to think that all that work went to waste!

ADDRESS Harvington Hall Lane, Kidderminster, DY10 4LR, www.harvingtonhall.co.uk TIP Neighbouring the hall, St Mary's Roman Catholic Church was built during the Catholic Emancipation, when freedom to practise the faith became enshrined in law (www.stmarysharvington.org.uk).

37 Home of *The Archers*

A load of old bull?

The Archers, a radio soap opera set in a village called Ambridge, has been running since shortly after the end of World War II rationing. The government wanted farmers to embrace change and increase productivity, and they thought a radio programme would be an effective educational tool. Of course, being on the radio means that *The Archers* is recorded in a studio that has little to do with its fictional setting, but it has long been thought that Inkberrow is the village on which Ambridge is based. Ambridge's pub, The Bull, could have been named after either of Inkberrow's pubs, The Bull's Head or The Old Bull, and the area has long been farming country.

It is unlikely that the people in the Ministry of Agriculture had any idea that their programme would win the hearts and minds of millions of listeners, many of whom are not involved in farming, or that it would still be running over 75 years later. The secret sauce? Probably the way that the programme reflects real life in rural areas, albeit a little more intense and sometimes ahead of its time.

It was not long after the show's inception that a storyline about an unplanned, out-of-wedlock pregnancy was aired. When the characters drank champagne to celebrate the birth of the child, the BBC received complaints about encouraging immoral behaviour. In the 1960s, the programme introduced organic farming and women outside 'traditional' roles. In the 1990s, the first Asian and first openly gay characters were introduced. In 2013, a three-year storyline was started about coercive control, which concluded shortly after this behaviour was criminalised.

All the rich tapestry of village and farming life is covered in the show, as it most probably is in Ambridge's inspiration, the village of Inkberrow. Visit one of the two Bull pubs, and you are sure to meet a range of interesting characters, all with stories to tell.

ADDRESS Inkberrow Village Green, WR7 4DY or Z (depending on which pub you choose) TIP The Bull Inn at Fernhill Heath between Worcester and Droitwich Spa is good for food – and, quite possibly, village gossip, too (www.thebullatfernhillheath.co.uk).

38 Medieval Moated Farm

A wealth of wildlife

Moats are probably best known as defensive features built around castles, but in medieval England, there were around 6,000 moated properties, not all of which were fortifications. In fact, a moat most likely signified wealth rather than a need for defence, and didn't necessarily form a complete ring. This well-preserved moat is one of at least four in the area and is likely to have surrounded a timber farmstead. The farm's fishponds are another indication of wealth and would have provided the family with an additional source of protein. They are thought to be 600 to 800 years old.

The neighbouring meadows' ridges and furrows indicate communal farming during a similar period. The whole village maintained large fields, and families had the right to farm multiple strips, each around an acre in size – an area that could be ploughed in one day. Each strip was worked by a team of oxen, starting in the middle and working clockwise. As the plough only turned sods to the right, this led to each family's strip rising in height to form a ridge in the middle, while the land between the strips reduced in height, creating a furrow. Today, the meadows are managed to maintain the pattern, with one cut for hay and the other grazed by sheep to create conditions attractive to a variety of wildflower species. In spring, the wooded areas are carpeted with primroses and bluebells.

The combination of woodland, meadows and water on the site provides a rich habitat for wildlife. The anthills in the grassland attract Green Woodpeckers to their favourite food – look out for their looping flight into the trees when they are disturbed. Marbled White butterflies float around the flowers in summer, their black-and-white checkerboard wings making them easy to identify. And, of course, dragonflies and damselflies flash shards of colour as they hunt the insects attracted to the flowers.

ADDRESS Inkberrow Millennium Green, Church Hill, Inkberrow, WR7 4DZ, www.inkberrowmilgreen.co.uk **TIP** One of the best moats in Worcestershire is around Birtsmorton Court. This 15th-century manor house is now a wedding venue available for private hire. The house and moat can be admired at a distance from the public footpath running to its south (www.birtsmortoncourt.com).

39 Bodenham Arboretum

No fairy-tale forest

The forests of fairy tales are dark, dangerous places, full of wolves and other scheming creatures lurking in the shadows, ready to munch on unsuspecting children for lunch. If that's what you expect when you head down to these woods, you are in for a big surprise! These trees were planted with love, designed to delight the eye and to commemorate people and events important to the Binnian family.

Even before deciding to open the arboretum to the public, the family's ambition was significant. First, they dammed the small streams running down the valleys to create no fewer than 15 ponds and lakes. The dam for the Big Pool alone took 12,000 tonnes of earth to create, and the stream took over six months to fill with 19 million litres of water. After the structural work was complete, it was time to focus on the trees. Since that first winter over 50 years ago, trees have been planted every year, creating a mosaic of interest across the site and the seasons.

In spring, rhododendrons and azaleas contribute vivid patches of colour. A little later, it is the laburnum tunnel that offers a high-vis experience. There are more trees that flower during the summer, and then come the cool, crisp days of autumn. Bright, sunny weather followed by an early frost makes the colours of the deciduous trees zing as their leaves turn, then drop, creating a crunchy carpet underfoot. And then, winter arrives. The skeletal silhouettes of the deciduous trees strike impressive poses in the watery light, but the evergreens can't help but take centre stage.

In all this profusion of growth, there is also a profusion of wildlife, skimming, darting, buzzing and padding softly through the undergrowth, although none of it is lurking, hiding behind trees and waiting to pounce on unsuspecting children – Bodenham Arboretum is altogether a different kind of fairy tale.

ADDRESS Wolverley, Kidderminster, DY11 5SY, +44 (0) 1562 852444, www.bodenham-arboretum.co.uk **TIP** If you enjoy visiting arboretums, there's another on the Arley Estate, just a 15-minute drive west of here (www.arleyestate.co.uk).

40 Severn Valley Railway

What's in a name?

Why do people have a tendency to name inanimate objects? Ships and boats are often named, from warships such as HMS *Victory* to ocean liners such as RMS *Titanic*, and canal boats named *Kingfisher*, to the autonomous underwater vehicle with a name chosen by public vote: *Boaty McBoatface*. Some locomotives are also given names. To some extent, they make the engine identifiable, although names, unlike serial numbers, can change. For example, the locomotive now known as *The Lady Armaghdale* started off life as *St John*, working on the Manchester Ship Canal. When it was bought by I.C.I., it was named after the chairman's wife. In 1993, it became *Thomas the Tank Engine* of children's storybook fame, and reverted to being *The Lady Armaghdale* in 2009.

What names also do is convey something about the object, and the values of those choosing the name. Pioneering railway companies realised that giving steam locomotives names made them more exciting, yet relatable to the travelling public. Who wouldn't want to travel on a train pulled by *The Rocket* or *Catch-Me-Who-Can*, when the alternative is a slow coach, pulled by horses?

Many locomotives on the Severn Valley Railway are named after naval ships, although those names sometimes convey other meanings too, for example, *Greyhound* and *Hercules*. One class of locomotives are all named after manor houses, perhaps conveying the idea of comfort and status. The locomotive in the photo is *Bradley Manor*, named after the medieval manor house near Newton Abbot in Devon that is now owned by the National Trust. It was introduced in 1938 as a lightweight option, at a time when some railway infrastructure could no longer support the weight of traditional locomotives. For most of its life, *Bradley Manor* operated in Wales, until it was withdrawn from service in 1965, after which it was refurbished by the Severn Valley Railway.

ADDRESS Station Drive, Kidderminster, DY10 1QX, www.svr.co.uk **TIP** Take the Severn Valley Railway, and you could visit a pub bearing the train's likeness on its sign, The Railwayman's Arms, which is on the platform at Bridgnorth.

41 Sir Rowland Hill Statue

Father of philately

Imagine a world where you had to pay to receive a letter, and that payment could be as much as a week's wages. Nowadays, we all take for granted how easy communication is, even to the point of filtering out countless unwanted messages. However, at the turn of the 19th century, the opposite problem existed. Sending a letter was so expensive that people resorted to using secret codes on envelopes, allowing the recipient to get the gist without paying for delivery.

In the absence of television and social media to distract him, Rowland Hill, born in his grandfather's house in Kidderminster, spent his spare time trying to work out a solution to this issue. He felt that if he could crack it, the postal system would be well used, gladden hearts, increase productivity and raise revenue for the government. Once he had developed his proposals, he sent them to the Chancellor of the Exchequer. Those with vested interests in the existing system opposed his 'preposterous' ideas, and no action was taken. In response, he printed his manifesto and distributed it to people outside the Post Office. Those without vested interests thought it was a good idea. *The Spectator* magazine adopted the cause, petitions were signed and representations were made to Members of Parliament. After less than three years of campaigning, the government capitulated and employed Hill to implement the new system.

Hill introduced the use of a postage stamp, which the sender of a letter would pay for at a standard rate, regardless of the distance the letter was sent. This started at just one penny, making it affordable for the masses. Within a year, the number of letters posted in the UK more than doubled, and within 10 years it had quadrupled. In quick succession, other countries adopted the idea, and within 20 years, stamps were used in 90 countries, gladdening many hearts around the globe.

ADDRESS 12 Vicar Street, Kidderminster, DY10 1DE TIP A blue plaque on 21 Blackwell Street marks Sir Rowland Hill's birthplace.

42 Papermill Cottage

From the pounding of rags to peace for bats

For around 200 years, this piece of land was home to a hive of industry, a far cry from what is here today. Until steam engines were introduced, the Industrial Revolution was powered by watermills such as the one that stood below Papermill Cottage, and paper was made from discarded cotton and linen rags. The papermill took partially broken-down rags and heated and pounded them to separate out individual fibres, creating a smooth(ish) slurry. This was lifted into a mould with a wire base and shaken backwards and forwards and from side to side to connect the fibres, then left to drain. The paper was turned out, then pressed between felted wool to remove as much moisture as possible before being hung up to dry. It was coated with gelatin to strengthen it, then dried and pressed again. The process used a lot of water and power, and created a lot of noise and pollution.

After a flood washed the mill away in 1852, it was not rebuilt, as the rag paper industry was on the wane. The cottage was lived in for another century, and then left to its own devices. Lesser Horseshoe bats moved in, and Worcestershire Wildlife Trust has secured the building and added nooks, crannies, bat lofts and bat boxes, making it more attractive to all sorts of bats. Of the 17 species of bat that live in Britain, 11 live on this nature reserve, feasting on the insects that thrive on its trees and wildflower meadows. And now they have another place to live and enjoy the peace of this now tranquil place.

For the best chance to see bats, visit around dusk from May to September. The entrance to the reserve is closed from 6pm. If dusk is later, turn left from the parking spots by the gate, then take the first road on the right and after about 760 yards, bear right onto a track that leads down to Leigh Brook. The footbridge takes you to the edge of Papermill Meadow.

ADDRESS Bridges Stone, near Alfrick, WR6 5HR, www.worcswildlifetrust.co.uk
TIP Another great place to see bats in Worcestershire is at Hurcott Pool, where the Worcestershire Bat Group has turned a boathouse into a bat hotel (www.worcestershirebats.org.uk).

43 Leigh Court Barn

The largest cruck barn in Britain

Leigh Court Barn was built for the manor of Leigh Court, when it was in the ownership of Pershore Abbey. The sheer scale of the barn gives an indication of the wealth of the monasteries and how much land they commanded. This is the largest remaining cruck barn in Britain, and one of the earliest.

Looking closely at the timbers, you will notice that the great, arching crucks are each made from the trunk of one tree, the shape determined by the natural shape of that tree. Commercial timber plantations now focus on growing trees as straight and tall as possible to create as little waste as possible in large-scale sawmills, but when this barn was built, the trees suitable for the crucks would have been chosen and felled for their curve. So, here we have 18 mature oak trees used for the crucks, plus many others used for the rest of the structure. You might also notice that no nails, screws, bolts or metal plates were used in the construction of the barn: it is held together by gravity and wooden pegs. It may seem like a primitive means of building, but the barn has stood for almost 700 years so far – carbon dating has shown that these trees were felled in the spring of 1344.

The barn would have been used to store all sorts of produce from the abbey's farms, including cereals. These were stored in sheaves until the grain or seed was needed. Then, they were taken to the stone-flagged section of floor, and the stone doors on each side were opened to create a through-draught. The harvest was threshed – beaten to separate the grain from the stalks – and then winnowed – lifted into the breeze to allow the dust and other debris to be blown away.

Of course, over the centuries, the way the barn was used changed. Brick walls replaced much of the wattle and daub, and a cider mill and press were installed at one end. Now, it is simply preserved for historical purposes.

ADDRESS Leigh, WR6 5LB, www.english-heritage.org.uk **TIP** Middle Littleton Tithe Barn is possibly even older, built from stone and designed to store the tithes (taxes) paid to the monks of Evesham Abbey (www.nationaltrust.org.uk).

44 Beacon Hill Toposcope

A sweet gift

Towards the end of the 18th century, the Lickey Hills were still wild and untamed – a far cry from how they are today. Things began to change when Birmingham expanded to the point that its residents sought greener places for recreation. When the 1871 Bank Holidays Act, which increased the number of bank holidays from four to eight, gave many more people the opportunity to take a trip into the countryside, the Lickey Hills became even more popular. However, at around the same time, common land on the hills was being enclosed. Visitors continued to arrive, but they had nowhere to go.

A combination of trespass, fence removal and a letter-writing campaign in the *Birmingham Post* resulted in the final 25 acres of Rednall Hill being purchased. A lease was negotiated with the landowner of Bilberry Hill, and a park incorporating both was officially opened in 1888. In 1907, the Cadbury brothers donated Beacon Hill, which was added into the park. At the end of the Bilberry lease, Birmingham Corporation purchased the land. Additional land was purchased and donated to the corporation up until the middle of the 20th century. Lickey Hills Park now covered 456 acres, 194 of which were donated by the Cadbury family.

Beacon Hill once housed a large iron basket that held a fire that could be lit to warn residents of an impending invasion, so they could muster a strong defence. Beacons were effective because each could be lit as soon as another was seen alight. This system was used to warn residents of the arrival of the Spanish Armada in 1588.

A toposcope was built on the summit in 1907 to commemorate the Cadbury family's gift of the land. In 1988, it was rebuilt and extended into a castellated structure. From here, on a clear day, if you can drag your gaze away from the impressive skyline of central Birmingham, you can see 13 old counties.

ADDRESS Beacon Hill, Birmingham, B45 9QH, www.birmingham.gov.uk
TIP Another beacon stood on Worcestershire Beacon above Malvern, and fires are sometimes still lit there to commemorate special events, such as Queen Elizabeth II's Golden, Diamond and Platinum Jubilees.

45 Bilberry Hill Range

The proof of the pudding is in the firing

If you imagine a carriage-mounted gun on the battlefields of World War I, then you probably have a reasonably accurate idea of what a howitzer looked like. Used between 1910 and 1942, howitzers were the army's go-to field gun because they were highly mobile and could fire at elevations up to 45 degrees. Although robust, howitzers and their carriages were sometimes damaged in battle. Towards the end of World War I, they were brought back from Europe to the Austin Motor Company factory in Longbridge, Birmingham, for repair and refurbishment. And rather than sending substandard and ineffective guns back to the front line, they needed to be tested before being returned to service.

Here in the Lickey Hills, an old quarry provided the perfect backdrop for a testing range. Concrete butts were constructed with a laminated wood-and-metal roof. They were given small side openings to allow some of the pressure to be released. Each butt was also partially filled with sand to prevent the cartridges and butts from being damaged. The cartridges themselves were rammed with more explosives than usual, known as a proof load. This put the guns under greater-than-usual pressure when fired, so any weaknesses in the repair work would become obvious.

Given the dangerous nature of this work, a concrete bunker was provided for the personnel to shelter in, and the guns were operated remotely. Because of the number of people employed, there were several buildings on site, including an engine house (now known as the School Room), barracks, a toilet block and a mess room. Most of these buildings have since been demolished, but it is still possible to see the remains of the magazine and the butts, by special arrangement, and some of the ammunition is on display in the visitor centre. The range is immediately opposite the visitor centre, and staff can advise on access.

ADDRESS The Visitor Centre, Lickey Hills Country Park, Warren Lane, Lickey, B45 8ER, www.birmingham.gov.uk/lickeyhills **TIP** The visitor centre does not have a café. However, there is one nearby – head back down to the main road and turn right, and you will find the Duckpond Cafe behind the Old Rose & Crown Hotel 600 yards along on the left (www.facebook.com/lickeycafe).

46 The Lickey Hoard

Receiving stolen goods?

If you had burgled a house and needed to distance yourself from the hot goods, where would you stash your swag? And what would you store it in to keep it safe? It would seem that one burglar in the 1970s decided that hiding their loot in a plastic carrier bag under a rhododendron bush was the right thing to do. It was another 40 years before the goods were recovered. By then, there was little chance of ever finding the owners, so they are now on display in the Lickey Hills Visitor Centre.

The hoard includes some cut-glass jars, one of which has a lid with a hole in the middle. From the late 19th century, these were common items on a middle-class woman's dressing table. Long hair was brushed for a few minutes every evening before bed to make it shine, and once done, the loose hairs caught up in the brush were removed and poked through the hole into the jar. When the hair receiver was full, the hair would be removed and sewn into a hairnet to form a pebble-shaped ball. These balls could be used to add volume when styling the remaining hair without adding too much weight. Considering that it was fashionable to grow your hair as long as you could, perhaps this was one way to make it appear longer than it actually was. It was not until the invention of the bob in the 1920s that women's hair started to be cut into shorter styles, leading to a reduction in the use of these storage devices.

The other pieces in the set may have held powder, hair grips and perfume, while the metal goods presumably came from elsewhere, as it would be unusual to store an icing nozzle and sugar spoons on your dressing table! The cut glass seems to have survived its unceremonious dumping in the woods, although some of the metal objects deteriorated in the damp conditions. As the sign with the goods says, this might not be a Saxon gold hoard, but it was still exciting to find!

ADDRESS The Visitor Centre, Lickey Hills Country Park, Warren Lane, Lickey, B45 8ER, www.birmingham.gov.uk/lickeyhills TIP If you are on the lookout for cut glass or other antiques, you could try Treasure Trove, an antiques dealer in Worcester (www.treasuretroveworcester.com).

47 Little Comberton

Domesday village

In 1066, the Duke of Normandy sailed across the Channel and soon gained his new title, William I of England – or, as he is better known, William the Conqueror. It did not take long for him to divide up the country among his supporters, and once that was done, he needed to refill his coffers. So he could understand exactly what assets he now had under his control and could therefore tax, he sent a team of inspectors across the country to create a record of the number of households, their status, and the land and resources available to them. Comberton was one of the places that was surveyed and included in the final record, known as the Domesday Book. This is the first real picture we have of life at the beginning of the Middle Ages.

Although all the land in the country officially belonged to the Crown, some was held by a tenant-in-chief, and some of their land was granted to the local lord, both grants being made in exchange for payment of taxes or the provision of military support. The land here was owned partly by Westminster Abbey and partly by Pershore Abbey, with none changing hands as a result of the conquest. However, the local Anglo-Saxon lords did change – they lost their entire land holdings in this area, although all of them retained some elsewhere.

The Comberton villagers were a mixture of enslaved people and smallholders who owned parcels of land. The enslaved did not own land and were considered to be possessions of the lords. The village also had a priest living here. The land included ploughland, woodland and meadow. There was also a watermill and a salthouse, both important elements of life at that time.

The village has a good collection of black and white houses, which date from around 500 years after the Domesday Book was written. This still makes them pretty ancient, and they give the village a lovely picture-postcard feel.

ADDRESS Little Comberton, WR10 **TIP** Every year in May, the village holds a 'Streetmarket', featuring games, stalls, morris dancers and live music (www.little-comberton.com/street-market).

48 Elgar's Grave

Journeying with Gerontius

Sir Edward Elgar's character and faith fashioned his music. He was brought up as a Roman Catholic in a Protestant society, and it is said that he always felt like an outsider. When he married Alice Roberts, one of his pupils – a published author and poet – her family even disinherited her because of his lowly status and Catholicism.

He took music lessons as a child, but his parents could not afford to send him to a conservatoire for formal training. So, he read every book he could, attended every concert he could and gained every experience he could to build his professional skills. It was not until he created *Variations on an Original Theme*, which became known as the *Enigma Variations*, that he became widely recognised for his talent as a composer. He was 42. Perhaps it was successful because it was such a personal piece, with each variation orchestrated to represent one of his closest friends. Another very personal work, *The Dream of Gerontius*, was a setting of John Henry Newman's poem of the same name. The poem explores the journey of the soul after death, as believed by Roman Catholics, so this choral piece was ill received by some in the UK, though it achieved critical acclaim across Europe. The works for which Elgar is probably best known are the *Pomp and Circumstance Marches*, which are central to the Last Night of the Proms, especially the trio (middle) section of the first march, 'Land of Hope and Glory'.

Ultimately a man of middle-class beginnings, Elgar gained global recognition and many awards and honours for his music, including honorary degrees and appointment as a Knight Commander of the Royal Victorian Order. He spent parts of his life in and around Malvern, and when he died, he was buried with his wife at this Roman Catholic church. Park on the road and walk down past the church. Turn right below the church and continue to the grave on the right.

ADDRESS St Wulstan's Church, Wells Road, Malvern, WR14 4JL, www.saint-wulstans.org.uk
TIP A statue of Elgar stands at the top of Church Street in Great Malvern.

49 Leper's Tile

'Have pity on me'

Now part of the Church of England, Little Malvern Priory was originally built for Roman Catholic Benedictine monks. The floor tiles date from the 15th century and were probably manufactured at Great Malvern Priory. Slabs of clay from the River Severn's floodplain were dried in the sun and then impressed with a pattern using a carved woodblock. The impressions were filled with liquid clay, known as 'slip', in a contrasting colour. Next came a lead glaze, which formed a honey-coloured skin over the slip and enhanced the clay's red hue when the tiles were fired in a kiln. Tiles made like this were so durable that these have survived for around 700 years, despite being on the floor.

The leper's tile is dated 1456 and bears an inscription from the Book of Job: 'Have pity on me, have pity on me, at least you, my friends, for the hand of the Lord has touched me.' By the time it was fired, leprosy in the UK was on the retreat. However, if you were unlucky enough to catch it, you would start by noticing a loss of feeling in your hands and feet. Slowly, this would lead to paralysis and ulcers. There was no cure, and after a while, your extremities would start to fall off, and your nose would probably collapse, leaving you with mucus running down your face. A papal decree dating from 1179 means you would be forced to wear a cloak and ring a bell as you walked around to warn others of your presence.

Leprosy was seen by many as a punishment for sin, and when the tile was fired, treatment would have revolved around improving a sufferer's spiritual life. St Benedict was known for his hospitality and caring for the sick, so finding a leper's tile in a monastery that lived by his rules is highly appropriate. These days, leprosy is curable and almost eliminated from Europe. However, over 200,000 new cases are still identified annually in other parts of the world.

ADDRESS Little Malvern Priory, Little Malvern, WR14 4JN, www.littlemalvernpriory.co.uk TIP India is one place where leprosy continues. Luckily, you can get a taste of India with no leprosy risk at the Marlbank Inn, about half a mile downhill from the priory (www.themarlbankinn.com).

50 Little Malvern Topiary

Protective peacocks

The garden of Little Malvern Court, and indeed the house itself, is open several times a year to raise money for charity, and both are well worth a visit. However, the topiary hedge on the western side of the garden can be enjoyed all year round from the public footpath, which runs down one side of the hedge.

It was the Romans who first introduced topiary to Europe, and like many other garden features, its popularity has waxed and waned over time, although not in a 'fast fashion' sense. The first revival lasted for a couple of centuries, and the second has been in play for a century and a half to date. Although this yew hedge looks as though it could have been in place for hundreds of years, the trees were only planted a century or so ago. Almost every part of the yew is toxic to humans, but they make ideal topiary trees because they grow bushy when cut back, have a long lifespan and have year-round deep green foliage. Yews have grown in the UK since the ice sheets receded, and are one of the country's three native conifers, with Scots pine and juniper the other two. The trees are particularly impressive in the winter months, when little else is in leaf, or frost or snow highlight the shapes they have been cut into.

Most of this hedge is cut into geometric shapes, but peacocks flank the gate into the garden. This is a common motif in topiary, as peacocks are associated with immortality and resurrection. This reputation is based on the idea that they have tough flesh, which is difficult to cook and resistant to decay. In the 5th century, Augustine notes that he left some cooked peacock flesh for over a year, and at the end of the period, it did not smell putrid; it was just a little shrivelled. Peacocks are often depicted guarding the gates of heaven, which makes them particularly appropriate to a garden surrounding a priory.

ADDRESS Little Malvern Court & Gardens, Little Malvern, WR14 4JN, www.littlemalverncourt.co.uk **TIP** For more formal topiary, head to Hanbury Hall near Kidderminster (www.nationaltrust.org.uk).

51 Tree of Knowledge

A crafty play on words

Madresfield Court has several claims to fame. It was the setting for Evelyn Waugh's novel *Brideshead Revisited*, which has since been adapted into a television series, film and audiobook. It was prepared during World War II as a place where the Royal Family could be evacuated if needed. It is also remembered by many for its maze, which has now been removed. And it was one of the places that Sir Edward Elgar visited as a child, while his father was tuning the pianos.

The house is also one of the best examples of the Arts and Crafts movement in Britain, which arose in opposition to mass production. The library shelving was installed in the early years of the 20th century. The ends of the bookcases are adorned with carvings of the Tree of Knowledge and the Tree of Life, created by members of the Guild of Handicraft. These are recognised as exemplars of the craft.

The Tree of Knowledge sports a top-hatted book thief skulking around the roots, with Adam and Eve standing above him. Eve is holding an apple, while other apples hang from the tree. The apple is a common symbol of the fruit of the Tree of Knowledge, although the Bible does not specify the tree's species. Apples are thought to have gained this rather unenviable reputation thanks to medieval scholars' love of word play: the Latin for evil is *malum*, and the Latin for apple is *mālum*.

Madresfield Court has another, altogether more positive, link with apples. For about 40 years, William Crump worked on the estate as the head gardener. During this period, he successfully crossed the Worcester Pearmain and the Cox's Orange Pippin apples. When he exhibited the result in 1908, this firm, crisp and juicy eating apple was awarded a Royal Horticultural Society Award of Merit. Although you are unlikely to see William Crump apples in the supermarket, the variety remains popular with gardeners.

ADDRESS Madresfield, WR13 5AJ, www.madresfield.co.uk
TIP The Madresfield Estate has a field-to-fork restaurant on Church Street in Great Malvern (www.madresfieldbutchersandgrill.co.uk).

52 Anne Darwin's Grave

Not a cure-all

To those who are not devotees of polar dipping, Malvern's Victorian hydrotherapy, known as the 'water cure', might seem like a strange idea that was just as likely to kill as cure. Patients were subjected to cold water wraps first thing in the morning, followed by an equally cold shower. After that, walking up onto the hills would have been a welcome way to feel warmer, although those too poorly to walk were allowed to take a ride on a donkey. At each spring along the way, known as 'wells' in this area, patients drank a glass of curative water. Malvern's water is famous, not for the minerals found in it, but for its purity – for containing nothing at all.

In 1849, Charles Darwin visited Malvern to partake in the water cure. He had been ill for some time, and traditional doctors had been unable to return him to health, so he thought it worth a try. After four months of treatment, his health had improved enough to travel home, where he continued with a watered-down version of the regimen. Having experienced the water cure for himself, he was convinced of its effectiveness, so when his beloved daughter Annie became ill the following year, they travelled from Kent to Malvern for her to receive the treatment. She stayed in Malvern for several months, but her health continued to decline, and she died on 23 April 1851. This was not the end of the water cure in Malvern, and influential Victorians, including Florence Nightingale, continued to flock to the town.

The craze for cold-water therapies gained traction again in the 21st century, although the scientific evidence for their effectiveness remains patchy. Whether or not it is valuable in the treatment of some conditions for some people, as its advocates suggest, it is certainly not a cure-all as, sadly, Charles Darwin learned when he lost his little Annie, whom he referred to as 'the joy of the household'.

ADDRESS Great Malvern Priory, Church Street, Malvern, WR14 2AY, +44 (0) 1684 561020, www.greatmalvernpriory.org.uk TIP Find out more about the water cure and Great Malvern's history at Malvern Museum on Abbey Road (www.malvernmuseum.co.uk).

53 Binidome

One of a kind

People in Malvern can still remember the day in 1977 when the Binidome was inflated; it does not look like an average building, and it did not rise like an average building! Bini was an Italian architect who developed a construction process that eliminated internal load-bearing walls and columns by mimicking the characteristics of an eggshell. Big or small, these buildings could be erected quickly and relatively cheaply, and the architect wanted the shape of this school sports facility to reflect the parabolic arc of a ball in flight.

A concrete sill forming the base of the dome was partially buried, and a neoprene layer was used to cover the ground in the middle. The builders placed steel reinforcing rods on top of this and then poured concrete mixed with plasticisers over them, followed by another membrane. For 90 minutes, they pumped air in underneath the concrete sandwich, and it slowly rose from the ground to form the shape you see today. After being allowed to set for 60 hours, the membrane was deflated, and holes were cut in the concrete to create the windows and doors.

This is one of only two Binidomes (also known as Parashells) ever built in England. The other has been demolished, leaving this as the only surviving example.

A moat was dug around the building to make it a more attractive venue for events other than just sports. Sound-deadening materials were used in the original construction, but the hall was still well known for a whisper on one side being audible on the other into the 2010s, when baffles were added to deaden more of the echo.

The building remains in use by Malvern St James School during the day, so its remarkable construction, topped with a now-green copper-alloy roof, is generally visible only from the road. However, some public fitness classes and sports training are held there in the evenings, if you would like to see inside.

ADDRESS Avenue Road, Malvern, WR14 3AG, www.msjsports.co.uk TIP To see another Grand Design, head over to 83 Old Hollow, West Malvern, which featured on the TV show in 2017. This is a private home, not open to the public – please be respectful of the occupants.

54 Bluebird Tea Rooms

An enigmatic time capsule

Every step you climb to the first-floor Bluebird Tea Rooms is like taking another step back in time, all the way to the early 20th century. Greeted at the top of the stairs, you will be shown to a table that could be the exact same table that composer Sir Edward Elgar sat at with his friend, Arthur Troyte Griffith.

The tea rooms opened in 1913, mere months before the onset of World War I. However, they survived those trying times and became a daily haunt of the architect Troyte Griffith, whose office was located above the nearby abbey arch. Although he was not a household name, visitors to Malvern will be familiar with his work, including the toposcope on the summit of Worcestershire Beacon. Troyte Griffith often met his good friend Elgar at the tea rooms. Each of Elgar's *Enigma Variations* was dedicated to and characterised one of his closest friends, including Troyte Griffith (Variation VII). As much of the furniture has not been replaced, it is quite possible that you will sit on the very chair that Elgar or Troyte Griffith sat on, or eat at a table they frequented.

It is also quite possible that you will be sitting at a table used by one of the boffins who flooded into Malvern during World War II to develop the radar technology that was critical in the Allies' victory in Europe. *Malvern's Secret War Heroes* by playwright Rachel Tobin recounts the locals' curiosity about these secretive strangers, who arrived during the war yet appeared to have no interest in the war effort.

Don't expect Scandi charm or baristas creating a heart on your latte here; the tea rooms have still barely changed since they opened over a hundred years ago. But the clientele certainly have, which begs the question not just of who once sat in that chair, but who is sitting in the tea rooms right now, and what contribution they might be making to life in the 21st century.

ADDRESS 9 Church Street, Malvern, WR14 2AA, +44 (0)1684 561166, www.bluebirdtearooms.co.uk, info@bluebirdtearooms.co.uk **TIP** If a modern coffee house is more your thing, try Abbey Road Coffee at the top end of the alley leading from Wells Road to the priory.

55 Donkey Shed

A cruel cure?

For centuries, donkeys were used to transport sick people to the healing wells of Malvern, but it was not until the water cure became fashionable in the 1800s that they became commonplace. Because many visitors were from areas with severe air pollution, the fresh air at the top of the hills was considered part of the cure. Although patients were encouraged to walk up, many were too sick (or possibly too lazy) to do so. Malvern air would not have been as clean then either, with quarries blasting dust into the atmosphere, significant construction projects generating additional dust, and a gasworks belching out smoke and noxious fumes. Although not ideal for the donkey, taking a ride to the top of the hills would reduce patients' exposure to this unhealthy concoction.

One of the first people to operate a donkey service from Happy Valley was Alice Betteridge's grandmother, who started in 1854. In a bit of tidy bookending, Alice herself was the last donkey handler on the hills, continuing in business until the 1940s. Every day, she walked her donkeys to Happy Valley from her home near North Quarry car park, and she would have used one of the donkey sheds here to shelter herself, her handlers and the donkeys from inclement weather. The drivers were typically young boys, beginning around age 6 and working until age 13. There were many cases of animal cruelty, including the overuse of whips and forcing donkeys to carry people too heavy for them. Some of this landed people in court, with punishments including fines and hard labour, although after the establishment of the Malvern Society for the Prevention of Cruelty to Animals in 1875, things improved – for the donkeys, at least. It was not until 1880 that schooling became compulsory for children aged 5 to 10, rising to 12 by 1899, thereby making full-time child labour impossible.

ADDRESS Just uphill from 36 St Ann's Road, Malvern, WR14 4RG **TIP** If you are unable to ascend the hills on foot, there is an all-terrain wheelchair-accessible route to the summit of Worcestershire Beacon leading up from Beacon Road car park. Electric 'Trampers' are available to hire from Cafe H_2O nearby (www.wyche-innovation.com/cafe-h2o).

56 Elmslie House

A flexible space

Since construction began on this house in 1862, it has had almost as many uses as owners. The architect Edmund Wallace Elmslie designed the house for his own occupation and began construction upon the completion of Great Malvern railway station and the Imperial Hotel (now Malvern St James Girls' School), both of which were also his designs. It appears that construction was still underway when he sold the house in 1866 to Archibald Weir, one of the doctors involved in the water cure. Weir finished the building and added his initials and the date 1867 to the north wall. In the 1880s, Weir also added a billiard room. Weir's family was followed by that of another doctor.

In 1927, Lawnside Girls' School bought the house and changed its name from St Mungho's to Lawnside Grove. It is thought that the final extension was built during the school's tenure, adding a stage at one end of the billiard room. This set the scene for the next phase of the building's life. It was bought by Philip Price, who used what was once the billiard room for concerts and parties, and dropped 'Lawnside' from the name. The violinist Nigel Kennedy is said to have played on this stage, and Philip Price married and lived here with cellist Julia Palmer (now Palmer-Price) and their children.

Since Anna Taylor and her family bought it, the house has been fully refurbished, retaining and enhancing many of the original features, and renamed again. The concert hall is used for concerts, art exhibitions and a twice-yearly craft market. Other parts of the house are used for jewellery workshops and as a yoga studio. The love that has gone into the building's renovation has given it a new lease of life and meant that it has remained a community space, as well as being a family home. Please respect the family's privacy and admire the house from the road, unless you are attending an event there.

ADDRESS 8 Avenue Road, Malvern, WR14 3AG, www.elmsliehouse.co.uk
TIP There is no longer a billiard table at Elmslie House. If you want to pot a few balls, you could try the Cue Corner in Worcester (www.thecuecorner.co.uk).

57 Gas Lamps

Multifaceted magic

Gas lamps might seem like nothing more than windows into the past. After all, they provided lighting to the dark streets of cities before the advent and rollout of electric lighting. Many people will associate gas lamps with centuries-old bridges across the rivers of European capital cities or their dim glow over the smog-bound streets of London.

Alternatively, if you grew up loving *The Chronicles of Narnia*, you might associate gas lamps with the gateway into a fantasy world. A world of speaking animals, mythological creatures, magic and spells. A world in which children can overthrow tyrants. A world in which a gas lamp stands just through the door in the back of a wardrobe. This world was created by C.S. Lewis, who was born in Ireland and schooled in Malvern, where he quite possibly learned to see the town's gas lamps as portals to a realm where he could create his own adventure.

As electric lighting became more commonplace and gas lamps became more expensive to maintain, Malvern's gas lamps were slowly removed. In 2001, Historic England saw the heritage value of those that remained and listed 27 of the 100 or so that were left, ensuring the future of these iconic structures in the town. However, that is not the end of the story, as in the 2010s, the gas lamps once again became significant, this time as a symbol of a better future. Transition Malvern Hills, a group set up to consider the town's transition away from reliance on fossil fuels as a response to global heating and climate breakdown, set up a team – the Gasketeers – to see what they could do with the gas lamps. The local council supported their work, and the project reduced the carbon footprint of each lamp by 80 per cent, shielded them to reduce light pollution, increased brightness, and lowered maintenance costs, all whilst retaining this important element of Malvern's heritage.

ADDRESS Throughout Great Malvern Town Centre and along Wells Road
TIP C. S. Lewis also frequented Malvern as an adult. His favourite pub was reported to be The Unicorn on Bellevue Terrace.

58 GBS Mulberry

The world's most travelled tree?

George Bernard Shaw spent considerable time in Malvern. He already knew the town when the Malvern Festival was established, initially for Birmingham Repertory Theatre to showcase his work, though it soon expanded to include other playwrights. The festival was so popular that Malvern's theatre was named after it. It ran annually from 1929 to 1939, then paused during the war and never regained momentum afterwards. The timing of the festival meant that Shaw often celebrated his birthday in Malvern. In 1936, his 80th birthday celebration was particularly special, as he planted a mulberry tree in Priory Park to mark the occasion. He reportedly said he hoped the tree would outlive him. And, indeed, it did.

Unfortunately, it did not live forever, though – in a particularly violent storm in 2000, this special tree was uprooted, causing great sadness among those who understood its value to the town's heritage. In response, some members of the Friends of Malvern Springs and Wells initiated a research project and found that cuttings of the tree had been sent to Malvern, Australia, in the 1950s. With help from the Australian authorities, they found that, although the cuttings had barely survived the journey, at least one of the trees was still thriving.

Six cuttings from that tree were taken in 2009 and flown back to Malvern, Worcestershire, where they were grown on. The strongest was subsequently replanted in the park, near the theatre and close to where the original tree had stood. The 2016 unveiling ceremony was attended by several people from Malvern, Australia, and locals, including a nonagenarian who had attended the original planting as a child.

Not only is this replacement tree, a progeny of the original, thriving, but it has also begun to fruit and, hopefully, it will continue to commemorate George Bernard Shaw's relationship with Malvern for many years to come.

ADDRESS Priory Park, Grange Road, Great Malvern, WR14 3HB
TIP Malvern still has a thriving theatrical scene, with world-class acts visiting Malvern theatres (www.malvern-theatres.co.uk).

59 Great Malvern Station

Speedy delivery

Compared to modern infrastructure projects, Great Malvern station was built in the blink of an eye. After the Worcester and Hereford Railway Act was passed in 1853, it took only seven years for land to be acquired, track to be laid, and the two stations in Malvern to be built and become operational.

Lady Foley, who owned much of the land in Malvern, was selling it off in parcels to provide accommodation to wealthy families who came here for the clean air on the hills and the pure water that poured from them. She helped fund the construction of Great Malvern railway station and, in exchange, was given her own private waiting room.

Despite the short timescales, it appears that no expense was spared in developing this significant new asset for the town. The station was designed by the renowned local architect Edmund Wallace Elmslie, alongside the hotel, which opened simultaneously and is now Malvern St James School. The sculpted stone and decorative metalwork were crafted by William Forsyth, based in Worcester, who had previously worked on Eastnor Castle and Witley Court. The large platforms are both covered by deep canopies supported by columns with intricate floral capitals made from brightly painted wrought iron.

The railway station played a key role in developing Malvern as a spa town. If you look near the ticket office, you will also see a large weighing scale built into the platform, and a Victorian post box was built into the station wall. This was a period of rapid technological change, but people still travelled to and from the station by horse-power, as shown by the horse trough built into the front wall of the station, now used as a flowerbed. Today, the trains probably serve more commuters to nearby cities than tourists, as the town's economy has shifted. This remains an active station, so please be careful while admiring the columns.

ADDRESS Station approach, Malvern, WR14 3AU TIP Malvern's other railway station, Malvern Link, neighbours Link Common, a popular place to stroll and picnic.

60 Green Man Misericord

A bit of comic relief?

Those familiar with church services that last about an hour once a week on Sunday might wonder why anyone felt the need to invent a misericord. However, a Benedictine monk would understand completely if he were expected to stand while singing the Divine Office. In St Benedict's Rule of the 6th century, he prescribed that the Divine Office be sung seven times each day and once at night, in addition to Mass and private prayer. During each of these, the monks were expected to stand, with the choir stall seat folded up behind them, spending hours on their feet every day.

At some point, a bright spark realised there was a solution to the discomfort monks were subjected to. They realised that if a small shelf were built underneath the seat, the monk could perch instead of standing, taking some of the weight off his feet. These little perches became known as 'misericords', and woodcarvers soon began decorating them. It was deemed inappropriate to carve biblical figures into something that would be sat on, so figures from folklore were often used instead.

Turn up the seats in Great Malvern Priory's choir stalls, and you will see a wide range of carvings. One depicts one of three Green Men in the priory. These are folkloric figures often depicted with their faces surrounded by leaves, or with leaves sprouting from their mouths, noses or eyes. However, here at Great Malvern Priory, the carving is of a face with a snake in its mouth. Little is known about Green Men, and people assign all sorts of meaning to them. Of course, being just faces, they might not even be men. Indeed, they were known as 'foliar heads' until they were renamed in the first half of the 20th century. Who knows what the carver of this head had in mind back in the 15th century when these seats were created, except for providing some relief – maybe even comic relief – for the monks?

ADDRESS Great Malvern Priory, Church Street, Malvern, WR14 2AY, www.greatmalvernpriory.org.uk **TIP** St Mary's church in Ripple (GL20 6HA) also has carved misericords, mainly depicting the months of the year.

61 Gullet Quarry

Blasted hills

The Malvern Hills Conservators, first granted powers by the 1884 Malvern Hills Act, sought additional powers to prevent the hills' total obliteration with increasing desperation as the quarrying of Malvern Stone became more industrial. Visitors to Malvern were beginning to despair of the noise and dust, and it seemed possible that the silhouette of the hills would be changed forever as quarrying continued. Some of the material was used for building, although it does not have straight planes, which means a lot of mortar must be used. However, the main use for the quarried stone was for the country's expanding road-building programme. Malvern Stone proved particularly useful due to its non-skid properties.

Gullet Quarry was the last one to finally close, in the 1970s. When operations ceased, the quarry filled with water from a spring, creating a lake that is approximately 16 feet deep and very cold. Despite this, or possibly because of the cool nature of the water, the quarry was a popular place for recreational activity until 2013, when two boys sadly met their deaths in its frigid waters. Since then, the quarry has been fenced, and authorities patrol the perimeter to try to control access for safety reasons.

The quarry is still worth a visit if you have any interest in geology, as it offers an exceptional exposure of Precambrian rock, formed over 540 million years ago, that meets Silurian geology, which is 100 million years younger. In the intervening periods, many features have formed, leaving a window into geological time. It is not only geologists you will find with binoculars trained on the rock face, as it provides a favoured nesting site for several species of birds. Whether or not you take your binoculars, it is worth climbing the path around the west side for the view past the rock face, over the water and out across the Severn Plain.

ADDRESS 270 yards uphill from Swinyard car park, Gullet Road, Malvern, HR8 1EU TIP If you continue straight past the quarry, through the woods, then continue ahead where the tracks cross, you will soon reach Eastnor Obelisk and be rewarded with views across Herefordshire.

62 Malvern Cube

From cradle to grave

When Worcestershire County Council announced its plans to close all its youth centres in 2010, the residents of Malvern were horrified. The youth centre was well loved and well used, and selling the land for housing to raise money did not seem like the best course of action for the town's young people.

A group of dedicated volunteers set up Malvern Community Collective and immediately started campaigning. The following year, after a lot of blood, sweat and tears, the council agreed to lease the building to the collective for 30 years at a peppercorn rent. Since then, a team of volunteers and staff has worked harder than ever, and Malvern Cube has gone from strength to strength. The Cube's ethos is to offer multi-generational, sustainable community services. Although there is plenty of youth provision, there are also all sorts of activities and events for older generations.

The café is popular, uses locally sourced produce, including that grown in the gardens outside, and keeps its prices as affordable as possible. The centre is home to over 30 community groups. Activities available include martial arts, exercise classes, dance, theatre, music and crafts. And if you have something broken, you can take it to the regular repair café, where skilled volunteers will endeavour to fix it for you. The large hall has a stage, so it is also used for performances. The concerts are wide ranging in style and often fully booked.

The charity that now runs the centre is focused on serving the community sustainably, which means it has a peace garden, growing space and a bank of rooftop solar panels, as well as social provision. This is a strong example of people power and a community taking things into its own hands, and is well worth a visit, whether simply for a cup of tea and a slice of cake or to join in one of the myriad activities on offer.

ADDRESS Albert Road North, Malvern, WR14 2YF, www.malverncube.com
TIP Malvern Library, another fantastic community space with a café, is just up the hill on Graham Road (www.worcestershire.gov.uk).

63 Malvhina

The only filtered spring in Malvern

The Malvern Hills are surrounded by springs, known here as 'wells'. Rainwater percolates down cracks in the ancient rock of the hills and wells from the ground where it meets an impermeable layer, creating streams, some of which are reliable and others of which come and go or change position. People from far and wide bring their water bottles to fill at the myriad taps and fountains fed from these springs.

Designed in 1998 by the sculptor Rose Garrard, the Malvhina spout reflects a triple theme of three. First, the water is taken from three sources: Happy Valley, Rushey Valley and Ivy Scar Rock. Second, three roads meet at this point. And third, the three significant periods in Malvern's development: that of the ancient Celts, the Dobunni tribe, who created and lived in forts on the Malvern Hills; that of the Benedictine monks, who established Christian communities here; and finally that of the Victorians, who turned Malvern into a fashionable spa town.

Although Malvern water is known for its purity, famously containing 'nothing at all', there are occasions when it becomes contaminated with agricultural waste. Only one of the wells is regularly tested and purified, using ultraviolet light and carbon filters, and that is Malvhina. Sometimes, that means there is a bit of a queue to fill a water bottle here. While you are waiting, you could walk along Belle Vue Island to admire the statue of Sir Edward Elgar or the stone sculpture representing his *Enigma Variations*. Alternatively, head south to admire his Banksy-style likeness using a mobile phone in the disused phone box below Rose Bank Gardens. The wait is worth it; the water is cool, refreshing and delicious – just what the doctor ordered!

Every year, Malvhina is decorated for the well-dressing festival over the May Day Bank Holiday weekend, along with around 50 other wells, fountains, taps and troughs.

ADDRESS Belle Vue Island, Great Malvern, WR14 4PZ TIP Usually held the weekend after the May Day Bank Holiday, the RHS Spring Festival takes place at the Three Counties Showground nearby (www.rhs.org.uk/shows-events/malvern-spring-festival).

64 Marvellous Trees

Serious status symbols

Walking up Avenue Road in Malvern from the railway station to the town centre, it is easy to be enchanted by the fairy-tale Victorian houses that line the street, standing in the middle of their garden plots. The multicoloured stone from the Malvern Hills, steeply angled roofs and decorative wooden soffits make many look as though they have stepped out of Hansel and Gretel's forest. If you can drag your eyes away from the beautiful houses, cast them skywards and take a look at the trees themselves. This is certainly not the dark, wolf-infested forest of fairy tales.

As Malvern was gaining in popularity as a spa town, Victorian plant hunters were scouring the globe and returning with exotic species. Having one of these trees in your garden was seen as a serious status symbol, and the wealthy Victorians who bought these new houses wanted the world to know how important they were. The trees they planted were only six to eight feet tall, nothing more than spindly saplings, but they signified something much larger. Is it possible that their owners had the foresight to see how these trees would have transformed the landscape of the town a century and a half later?

Now, everyone who visits Great Malvern has the opportunity to admire giant sequoias, cedar trees, Corsican pines, holm oaks, monkey puzzles and many more spectacular, mature trees. The whole town from Great Malvern railway station up Avenue Road, through Priory Park and the Priory churchyard, then up onto the hills, is like a public arboretum.

The trees now frame the houses and the skyline. Some produce enormous, phallic cones. Some pop like firecrackers on a hot summer's day. And some just go about their business quietly, growing and extending their branches to offer shade, providing a home to wildlife and cooling a heating planet. Long live Malvern's marvellous trees!

ADDRESS Avenue Road, Malvern, WR14 3AR TIP If you would like to know more about Malvern's marvellous trees, you can pick up self-guided walk booklets at the tourist information centre (Lyttleton Well Courtyard, WR14 2AY).

65 Morgan Experience

Uncompromising in craft

In the late 1980s, the leading industrialist Sir John Harvey-Jones visited the Morgan factory in Malvern for the BBC's *Troubleshooter* series. He was astonished at what he saw: a process in which the wheels were added to the car first so it could be pushed around the factory, both uphill and downhill, with everything done by hand. Only nine cars were made each week, and the lead time for orders was extraordinary. Sir John recommended large-scale, immediate change, which the Morgan family, steeped in tradition, resisted. This became one of the most-viewed episodes of the series, driving the waiting list up even further!

Ten years later, Sir John revisited the site and found that the family had listened, considered his advice and made several changes. For example, aluminium was now cut by laser rather than by hand, and the workshops were now organised so the cars were only pushed downhill, and not back up.

Since then, many more changes have been made to the factory – and these can be seen close-up on the Morgan Experience tour. Morgan cars are still made by skilled craftspeople who undertake a five-year apprenticeship. It still takes 13 hours to form an ash frame (using British ash), 7 hours to hand-shape a bonnet and 38 hours to tailor an interior. Now, all this is done in a clean factory that follows lean manufacturing processes, where you can see every stage of production.

At the Morgan Experience, you can get up close and personal to these icons of British motoring and see for yourself the expertise of the Morgan workshop teams. If you are itching to get behind the wheel, you can hire a car or take an experience drive. And, of course, it is also possible to buy a new Morgan, customised to your personal tastes. You will still need to wait, but your patience will be rewarded with a handcrafted car that is beautiful, unique and fun to drive.

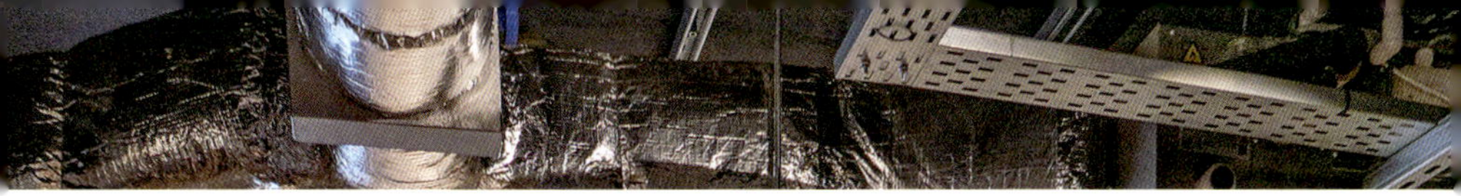

ADDRESS Spring Lane, Malvern Link, WR14 2LS, +44 (0) 1684 573104, www.experience.morgan-motor.com, experience@morgan-motor.co.uk TIP The Morgan Experience café, run by local company FAUN, serves a small selection of treats. For FAUN's full range of meals, head up to their café at 31–33 Worcester Road (www.faunmalvern.co.uk).

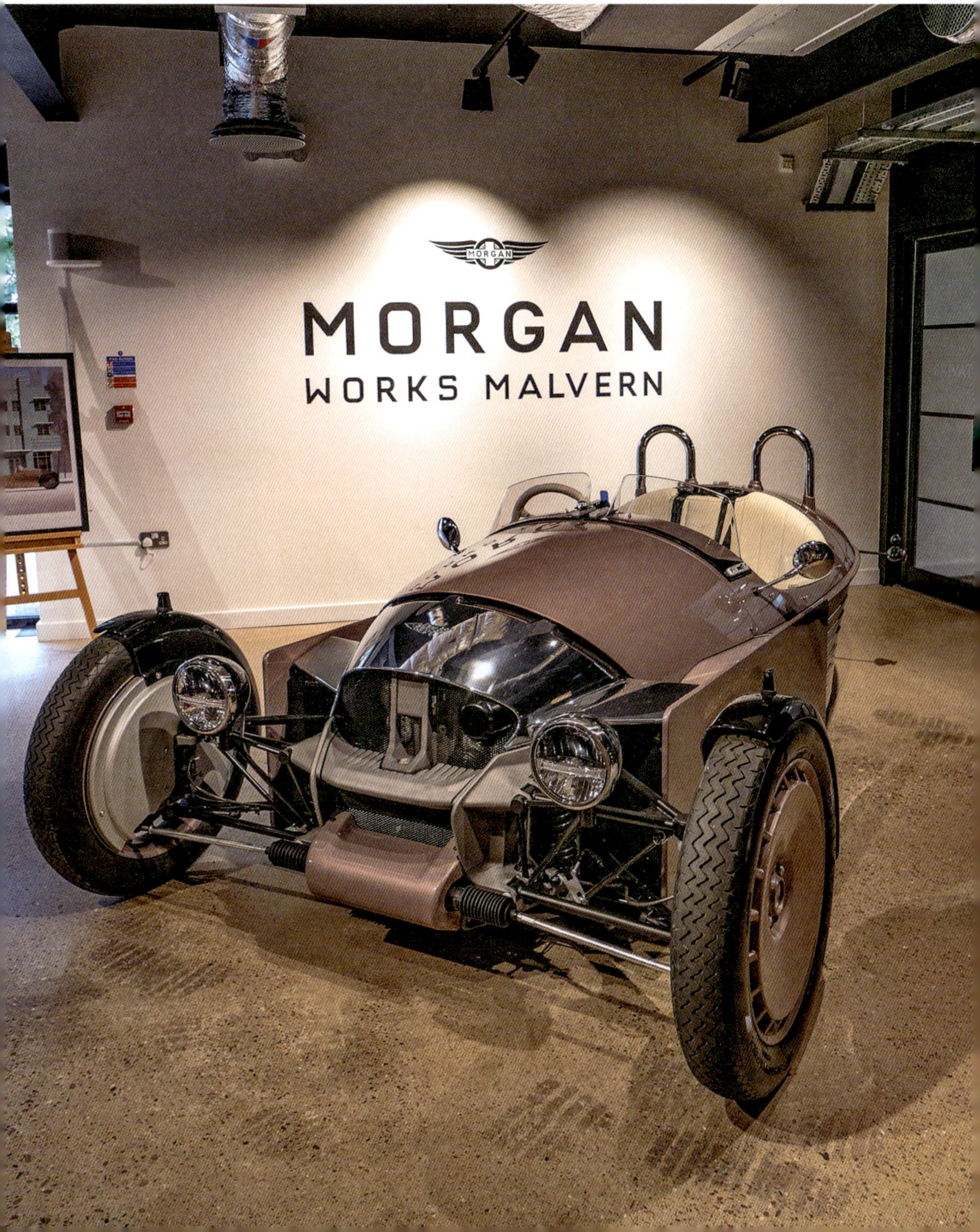

66 Rose Bank Gardens

The secret is in the sauce

It would be wholly inappropriate to write a book about Worcestershire without mentioning one of its most famous exports: Worcestershire Sauce. Several legends surround the origin story of this deeply umami condiment, possibly helping to increase its intrigue and appeal to purchasers. One story that, true or not, has stuck is that Mr Lea and Mr Perrins, both chemists in Worcester, invented the sauce in the 1830s, but it was totally inedible. They set what they had made aside and continued their experiments until they ran out of storage space. Some 18 months later, they tried the sauce again – and it was now delicious! A family fortune was made.

Two generations later, Charles William Dyson Perrins was running the family business and lived in a Regency house called 'Rose Bank' in Great Malvern, which he gifted to the town in 1918. The town council demolished the house the year following his death, maintaining the land as a public garden, with lawns and flower borders, and fabulous views.

The gardens also boast a couple of spectacular steel sculptures by Herefordshire artist, Walenty Pytel. One is of a pair of buzzards. The other is of a solitary skylark, rising high into the sky. Both birds are common around the Malvern Hills. Keep an eye out for a large bird of prey, wheeling above the town and emitting an occasional cry. If it doesn't have a forked tail, it is likely to be a buzzard (if its tail *is* forked, it's a red kite). Skylarks are more likely to be heard than seen, singing their staccato song high above the meadows that flower lower down the slopes. The birds are small and fly so high that they can often not be seen against the expanse of sky.

We may not know the real origin story of Lea and Perrins' Worcestershire Sauce, and the full ingredient list may remain a secret, but the Perrins' legacy lives on, in our food and this park.

ADDRESS Wells Road, Malvern, WR14 4RQ TIP Malvern has a plethora of public parks. For one nearby, where bands use the bandstand in summer, head to Priory Park behind Malvern Theatres.

67 Swan Pool

Fish on Fridays

When Malvern Priory was established, it belonged to London's Westminster Abbey, an order of Benedictine monks. The Catholic Church forbade anyone to eat meat on Wednesdays, Fridays, Saturdays or during Advent or Lent, to honour Jesus and the sacrifice of his flesh for everyone else. Benedictine monks had further restrictions on their consumption of meat from four-legged animals.

Non-meat days accounted for around half the year, which meant there was a significant demand for alternative sources of protein. As 'meat' in this context meant anything hot-blooded, fish and shellfish did not fall into this category and became a mainstay of monastic diets. Much sea fish that made it to inland monasteries such as this was preserved by salting or drying, and not always very flavoursome as a result. Many monasteries had ponds or lakes to provide fresh fish. It is thought this is how Swan Pool in Priory Park started its life, and it may also have been used to rear two-legged animals such as ducks and geese.

During the Victorian era, the pool became part of the garden of Priory Mansion, and it is now part of Priory Park. For a while, it was used as a boating lake, but in recent years, the focus has shifted towards wildlife conservation. When the pool was renovated in 2022, it still contained fish – 30,000 of them – but they were generally in poor health. The pool was desilted, and marginal plants were placed at one end to provide a more varied habitat for invertebrates, amphibians and fish. The upper pool has been left fish-free to give frog and toad spawn a better chance of survival, and the lower pool was restocked with roach, rudd and perch. You won't find any monks on the banks with fishing rods these days, although if you are lucky, you might spot a kingfisher on the specially designed perch, patiently waiting for dinner to appear below.

ADDRESS Priory Park, Great Malvern, WR14 3DR **TIP** Locals debate which is the best fish and chip shop in Malvern. There are two good options in Barnard's Green, at the bottom of Avenue Road.

68 Technology Station

Boffin brilliance

Malvern is brimming with boffins. It started with a tidal wave when the Telecommunications Research Establishment, where the phrase *boffin* originated, and the Air Defence Research and Development Establishment were moved to Malvern in a bit of a hurry in 1942. At the end of the war, the establishments remained, and the boffins settled in. This century, the number of boffins has ebbed, but the defence technology company QinetiQ remains an important employer, so plenty remain.

Although much of QinetiQ's work is confidential, some of its predecessors' work is now in the public domain. Malvern is well known as an important centre for radar development. One place where new radar technology was crucial was the Battle of the Atlantic. This battle lasted the entire duration of World War II, beginning with the Allied blockade of Germany and Germany's retaliatory blockade of the Atlantic shipping lanes essential to the supply of food and raw materials to Britain. Until microwave airborne radar was invented in Malvern, German U-boats picked off ships in convoys like sitting ducks. Afterwards, the attrition rate dropped like a stone.

After the war, research continued. The team here revolutionised screen technology with liquid crystal displays and touch sensitivity. They developed infrared technology, which allows emergency services to navigate in dark and smoky conditions, switches on your garden light and enables heat-seeking missiles. And they invented surface acoustic wave devices – an essential element of mobile phones.

The technology station showcases these and many more examples of the importance of the research establishments in Malvern. Many of the volunteers who run the museum are retired boffins themselves – if you would like a detailed explanation, they might just be able to provide it, or know someone who can.

ADDRESS Great Malvern railway station, Malvern, WR14 3AU, www.mraths.org.uk
TIP Many of the early displays in the museum were first shown on Great Malvern Exhibition Walk, a series of display cases that run down the side of Waitrose and into the town centre. What's on display there right now?

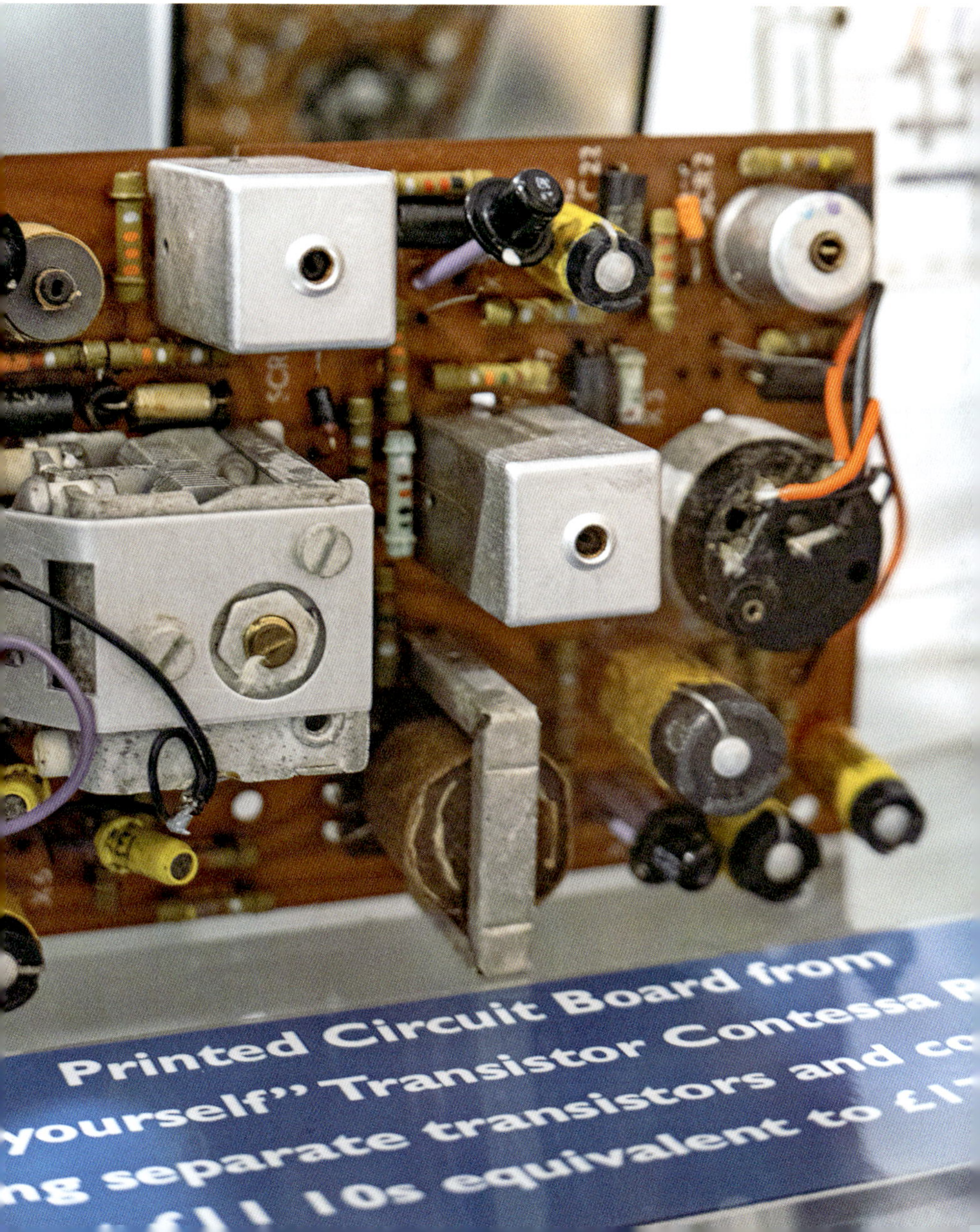

69 Worcestershire Beacon

The highest point in Worcestershire

The Malvern Hills rise from the undulating Severn Plain like the back of a sleeping stegosaurus, in a line that runs almost exactly north to south. Although not particularly high, these hills feel mountainous because of their prominence in the landscape. Worcestershire Beacon is the highest of the hills, rising to 1,394 feet.

From the top, the views are stupendous. On the horizon to the north, Long Mynd also stands proud against the rest of the landscape. On cold winter days, it becomes more obvious when covered in a sprinkling of snow. Turning to the north-east, the Lickey Hills can be seen in the distance, and continuing clockwise, the whaleback of Bredon Hill swells up alone on the far side of the River Severn. Just to its south, the Cotswolds Escarpment rises steeply from the plain and disappears into the distance. Looking all the way to the south, along the line of the hills past the ridged outline of British Camp Iron Age hill fort, on an exceptionally clear day, it is possible to catch the glimmer of the Bristol Channel. Turning again, the Herefordshire hills rise in the west to meet the mountains of Wales. A toposcope stands on the summit so you can distinguish one feature from another.

This is an excellent place to watch weather patterns march across the landscape and catch a glorious sunset on a clear summer evening. Because of the hills' prominence, it is almost always windy at the top of Worcestershire Beacon, and the temperature is usually two or three degrees lower than in Malvern. It is a good idea to take one more layer of clothing, preferably windproof, than you think you will need. The easiest way to reach the summit is from the Upper Beacon Road car park, from where a track gently rises all the way. If you rely on wheels for mobility, you can hire an all-terrain scooter from Cafe H_2O near the car park that can take you all the way to the top.

ADDRESS Upper Beacon Road car park, Malvern, WR14 4EH
TIP The Malvern Hills GeoCentre is a great place to learn about the geology of the Malvern Hills (www.wyche-innovation.com).

70 World's Tiniest Theatre

Making a big splash

Malvern grew in popularity as a spa town at about the same time that urinating and defecating in public were beginning to be seen as socially unacceptable health hazards. Indoor flushing toilets were also starting to replace outhouses, so this was the era in which public toilets started to be provided in urban areas, including this one, servicing Malvern's town centre.

Recognised by Guinness World Records, it now houses the world's smallest commercial theatre, but how could it possibly have been so small in the first place, even as a public toilet?

The answer is associated with a phenomenon known as the 'loo leash', designed to keep women out of the public realm; public toilets were provided only for men. This impacted women in the lower socio-economic classes the most, as they could not use the toilets that were beginning to be provided in the department stores and tea rooms that only catered to middle- and upper-class women. Public toilet provision in the UK today still favours men, despite over a century of campaigning.

Luckily, neither men nor women out and about in Malvern need to rely on this public toilet any longer. And even more luckily, it has been converted into a quirky little theatre – the Theatre of Small Convenience. Originally founded by Dennis Neale in the late 1990s, it closed when he retired and was fully refurbished and reopened in the 2020s, thanks to the dedication of a small team of volunteers and several charitable grants. The theatre only seats 12, and the usher has to stand outside, whatever the weather. Inside, it is comfortable and does not smell as you might fear. The stage is as tiny as you might expect, so performers have to be creative about how they use the space. Those who have unleashed themselves and risen to the challenge include poets, musicians and a human worm. Yes, you read that right: a human worm!

ADDRESS 3 Edith Walk, Malvern, WR14 4QH, www.smallesttheatre.org
TIP Great Malvern is well furnished with theatres. The Coach House Theatre is also quite intimate, seating up to 100 people and hosting a range of performances (www.coachhousetheatre.co.uk).

71 The Worm

Early disabled access

Spa mania was at its height when the railway arrived in Great Malvern. Dr Gulley, purveyor of the water cure, was involved in the establishment of the Imperial Hotel, which opened at the same time as the station. Some claim it was the largest in Western Europe at the time of construction, and a contemporary report in the local newspaper described the hotel as magnificent; and, as one of the first to be lit by incandescent gas, it would certainly have been impressive, even in the hours of darkness.

The railway brought visitors to Malvern from smoky, polluted cities to take both the air and the water. Many of those visitors were not in the best of health and travelled to Malvern to seek a cure for their ailments. If you stand on the road bridge next to the station and look north, you will notice a corrugated iron roof snaking from the bridge towards the hotel, which is now Malvern St James girls' school. This provided a covered walkway so that, on arrival, guests would not have to endure the discomfort of inclement weather before checking in. The worm also offered a gentle slope to the level of the hotel, making the approach easier for guests who were infirm – a very early example of disabled access, which is one of the reasons the worm is Grade II listed. Of course, a visit to Malvern was expected to cure patients of infirmities, so the journey to the station for the return train had to be made outside or in the comfort of a carriage.

A little beyond where the worm disappears under the hotel, there is a set of doors. This was another entrance to the hotel, used for delivering goods. Primarily, this was used for coke for the hotel's boilers and saline water from Droitwich Spa to enable guests to bathe in brine, as well as Malvern water, which famously contains nothing at all.

These days, the worm is considered unsafe, so it is closed at both ends, and best seen from above.

ADDRESS Avenue Road, Malvern, WR14 3BA (the worm can be viewed from the bridge over the railway, looking north) **TIP** The spirit of the Water Cure lives on in Malvern in a cocktail and coffee bar by the same name. Continue to the top of Avenue Road, turn left, and you will find it on the crossroads in the town centre (www.thewatercure.co.uk).

72 Holywell

Holy mackerel! It contains nothing at all!

Holywell is purportedly the first place in the world to bottle water; this was done by the monks of Great Malvern Priory as early as 1622, so they could give the purest possible water to the elderly or infirm. They seemed to know something that was proved scientifically in 1743 – that, unlike mineral waters, which contain inorganic elements dissolved from the rocks they pass through, Malvern water contains nothing at all, except hydrogen and oxygen.

When Schweppes took over the bottling in 1850, they seem to have concluded that this was not enough. First, they carbonated it – and sold it as Malvern Soda at the Great Exhibition of 1851, where Queen Victoria was introduced to its delights, thereby earning it a royal warrant. Later, Schweppes added chlorides as well as carbonates, so that it would match the profile of the natural spring water from the village of Niederselters in the Duchy of Nassau in Germany, from which the word 'seltzer' is derived, and which was proving very popular in fashionable circles. They called this Malvern water with additives 'Malvern Seltzer'. Towards the end of the century, Schweppes moved production to a spring on the west side of the hills in Colwall, where they continued to operate for over 100 years.

Bottling continued at Holywell until the 1960s, and the well building was restored in 1979. However, the lack of space at the site and the narrow access road do not make it very attractive for modern production and distribution, so it was not reopened for bottling until 2008. This time, Holywell Spring Water has nothing added, except carbonation for the sparkling variety. It is, once again, as pure as when it leaves the ground, and, having risen through cracks in the ancient igneous and metamorphic rocks of the Malvern Hills, which are not water soluble, once again contains nothing at all. Except hydrogen and oxygen, of course.

ADDRESS Holywell Road, Malvern Wells, WR14 4LE, www.holywellmalvernspringwater.co.uk **TIP** To buy a bottle of Malvern Holywell Spring Water, try looking in Waitrose in Great Malvern.

73 St Wulstan's Nature Reserve

A glowing transformation

Today, St Wulstan's Local Nature Reserve is a peaceful haven for plants and wildlife, but that was not always the case. In the lead-up to the D-Day landings, part of Brickbarns Farm was requisitioned for a hospital to care for American soldiers involved in the campaign. Nissen huts and low brick buildings sprang up across the site. Almost overnight, fields were transformed into something resembling a small town, including hospital wards for servicemen suffering from shell shock (now known as post-traumatic stress disorder), staff accommodation and other facilities such as a gym, concert hall, chapel and library. There were also gardens, orchards and allotments, and residents recall seeing glow-worms, despite all the activity.

After the war, the site was used as a camp for European Volunteer Workers, mainly displaced from the Baltic states. After that, it was repurposed as a tuberculosis hospital until antibiotics rendered it obsolete. The site was again repurposed, this time as a psychiatric hospital, which was internationally recognised for its rehabilitation of patients, at a time when few were ever discharged once admitted.

The introduction of Care in the Community was the catalyst for the next major change. The hospital buildings were no longer needed and had fallen into disrepair. They were demolished, and part of the site was developed for housing, with the rest transformed into a local nature reserve. To honour the site's history, the exotic trees and plants and some of the garden boundaries have been retained. Combined with new meadows, it is delightful for both human visitors and wildlife.

And throughout all of this, the glow-worms have remained. For a chance to see them, take a walk through the reserve on a calm evening in June or July, with a crescent moon lighting your way, and look out for the glowing green females in the grass.

ADDRESS St Wulstan's Drive, Malvern Wells, WR14 4JA TIP St Wulstan's was one of 14 Worcestershire hospitals that treated almost 80,000 American soldiers. Blackmore Park hospital's water towers are still standing next to the road to Blackmore Park Industrial Estate.

74 Plague Stone

Forsaken but not forgotten

The early days of the COVID-19 pandemic were terrifying. The medical establishment did not know the most effective way to treat the disease or reduce transmission within the population. All they knew was that it was contagious, and it was killing people.

Imagine a similar scenario 700 years ago, when the bubonic plague was sweeping across the country. An understanding of bacteria was centuries away. Communication was not fast or reliable. People were dropping like flies, at first suffering a fever and then vomiting blood for hours to as much as three days before they died. Later outbreaks were weaker; people lived for long enough to develop boils and black buboes – swollen, inflamed lymph nodes – before they died.

So many people perished that churches stopped ringing their passing bells to try to quell panic. But the population knew intimately how scary this was, how many people were dying, because they were seeing it with their own eyes. And for many, it felt like their God had forsaken them.

But they did not forsake each other. People still needed food and other supplies, and although the medical and scientific establishment had no idea how the plague was transmitted, some thought it was spread by human contact. The concept of the plague stone was born – somewhere coins could be deposited in vinegar to pay for goods that were left for villagers to pick up, with no human interaction required.

Unlike COVID-19, it took over 500 years for researchers to determine the cause and means of transmission of the bubonic plague, and in the meantime, the population had to learn to live with it. This plague stone is evidence that the people of Ombersley were not cut off during those times when infection hit; although it did not help with infection control, it does at least indicate that others cared enough to continue supplying affected villagers with essential goods.

ADDRESS Ombersley crossroads, Ombersley, WR9 **TIP** Just a few yards south on the A4133, Checketts is a popular local coffee shop.

75 Avon Meadows

Flooded with wildlife

The floods of 2007 will go down in Worcestershire's history as among the worst ever recorded. The River Avon was 15 feet above its usual summer level, but it was not only the river that caused devastating flooding in the town. Part of the issue was the inability of small watercourses and street drainage to cope with prolonged, heavy rainfall. In consultation with the local community, the councils came up with a solution – a nature reserve with 24 hectares of floodplain meadows. Pools and scrapes were dug, drains were diverted, and 50,000 reeds were planted by local people. Now, when it rains heavily, the runoff flows into the wetlands, where some is used by plants, it is cleaned by reeds, and it slows down on its way to the river. A boardwalk and paths cross the meadows.

In winter, the reserve can be covered with floodwater for weeks at a time. Many plants die back, but evergreens such as holly and ivy offer winter colour, and nectar and berries for wildlife. Overwintering birds paddle around, and everything prepares for spring, when all the plants start regrowing. Yellow flag irises and marsh marigolds add flashes of colour along the water's edge, and buttercups begin to bloom in the meadow. With the flowers and warmer weather, the reserve comes alive with insects, in time for the arrival of summer birds, including cuckoos, swallows, martins and swifts. Look closely at ground level, and you might spot tunnel runs for small mammals trying to navigate the area without being seen by predators. And look up as the day begins to darken to see bats flitting around, feasting on insects.

As the days cool and the bats hibernate, the winter birds arrive. The resident starlings congregate at dusk, forming great swirling masses that fly together in a murmuration, creating fantastical shapes until – seemingly at the flick of a switch – they all drop to their roosts.

ADDRESS King George's Way, Pershore, WR10 1EY, www.avonmeadows.org.uk
TIP The Wychavon Way long-distance path runs through Pershore. For more opportunities to see local wildlife, try walking the section from Pershore to Broadway. It's a long day out – 17 miles of walking – but with plenty of places to relax when you arrive.

76 Confetti Flower Fields

Sublime summer scents

For centuries, people across the globe have practised the bizarre ritual of throwing small items over each other at times of celebration. Over time, the rice, grains, mud and rotten fruit have been replaced with confetti – altogether a more desirable alternative for those in the firing line. In the 1970s and '80s, wedding confetti consisted of small pieces of pastel-coloured paper, which, much to the chagrin of the authorities, collected in the corners of church steps. By the 2000s, metallic confetti had made a glittering entrance, finding its way into weddings, table decorations and Christmas cannons. Venues hated this even more, as the small pieces are so difficult to clear up and, as they are made from plastic, litter the environment for thousands of years.

The time was right for the growth of confetti made from real flowers. The dried petals flutter delightfully in the breeze and simply biodegrade naturally if they are not cleared up, giving nutrients back to the earth rather than polluting it. Many venues now specify that confetti must be made only from flower petals. Add in the health benefits of time spent in nature and the population's love of taking photos on our phones, and you have the perfect timing for an experience that combines all these factors.

Since 1997, the Wyke Manor Estate has been growing flowers and making beautiful, biodegradable confetti. And now, for two magical weeks a year in June/July, the fields are open to the public to experience the bliss of wandering through this fragrant mass of flowers. Stripes of colour ribbon across the field, with people wandering along the mown pathways, their heads just visible above the tall stems of the delphiniums, whose dried petals have the perfect confetti flutter.

For flower lovers, this is a sublime experience. For families, a perfect photo opportunity. And for couples, a decidedly romantic date.

ADDRESS Wyke Manor, Wick, Pershore, WR10 3NZ, +44 (0) 1386 555045, www.confettidirect.co.uk, info@confettidirect.co.uk **TIP** If you want to grow your own delphiniums, Mill Lane Nursery in Drakes Broughton may well have some in stock (www.milllanenursery.co.uk).

77 Peregrine Palace

Exhilarating ringing

Peregrine falcons are the fastest animals on Earth. They are specially adapted to withstand speeds of up to 200 miles per hour, enabling them to keep their eyes open while dive-bombing for dinner. They are predatory, territorial and fiercely protective parents, so it is no wonder that the trained and licensed handlers who remove their young from the platform on Pershore Abbey wear hard hats – not to protect them from falling, but from attack by the parents. The young are weighed and have rings placed around their legs to help us better understand these incredible birds, before they are returned to their nests. What a scary process for the ringing team, even without the abseil down the tower to reach the platform!

The other ringing team – those who ring the church bells – also has an exhilarating time. By the 19th century, the abbey church's structure was in severe decline, so the Victorians embarked on a major refurbishment. The architect involved, George Gilbert Scott, was so taken with the panelling in the top of the tower that he wanted to make it visible to the congregation. This meant removing the ringing floor and replacing it with a unique diamond-shaped platform, suspended high in the tower. To reach it, the ringers embark on an adventurous journey up a stone spiral staircase, through the roof space, along passages, and then up a vertiginous open metal staircase near the top of the tower.

Visitors to the abbey can listen to the bells being rung most Sundays, and the tower is occasionally open to intrepid members of the public. You can watch the peregrine chicks develop from fluffy balls of cuteness to sleek killing machines over the course of a month or so in spring. Take binoculars to watch from the ground or check out the webcam footage online. No hard hats are needed – when not feeling threatened, these birds are more interested in pigeons than people.

ADDRESS Pershore Abbey, Church Walk, Pershore, WR10 1BL, +44 (0) 1386 552071, www.pershoreabbey.org.uk, www.youtube.com/@PershorePeregrines-qj9qo **TIP** Peregrine falcons can also often be found nesting on the Malvern Hills quarry faces.

78 Powick Mills

First municipal hydroelectric power station

Here in Britain, we have been harnessing the power of water for around 2,000 years. Water mills ground wheat into flour and powered industrial processes, such as weaving, long before we developed methods to generate electricity from it. The first house to be powered by hydroelectricity was Cragside in Northumberland. It took another couple of decades for that process to be scaled to such an extent that it could power a whole city – and the first city to benefit was Worcester.

Powick Mills had been used for various purposes since their inception, and in 1894, turbines were placed over the water to generate electricity. To much celebration, the main roads in the city were lit. The large chimney that still stands rose from the steam boiler that was added to the site to be used either as a back-up or top-up facility.

It wasn't long before the introduction of electric trams in the city meant that demand for electricity outstripped the supply capacity of Powick Mills. Consequently, a steam-powered station was built on Hylton Road. This gradually replaced the hydroelectric facility, and Powick Mills stopped production in the 1930s.

These days, Powick Mills are private apartments, and hydroelectric schemes tend to be either fairly small-scale and community-based or massive pump-storage facilities. The former produce electricity fairly consistently, although they can suffer from technical challenges, particularly when source rivers flood. The latter use electricity when the grid has plenty to spare to pump water to a high lake. Then, when there is not enough power in the grid, the water is released through the turbines to balance supply and demand. This process is flexible enough to support the expansion of solar and wind energy, ensuring the lights stay on across the country even when the wind is not blowing and the sun is not shining.

ADDRESS Old Road, Worcester, WR2 4BU **TIP** Hydroelectric power is not a thing of the past in Worcestershire. Pershore Leisure Centre is powered by turbines on the neighbouring River Avon (www.riversfitness.co.uk/pershore).

79 Sacred Sharpening Stone

Desperate desecration

The British Civil Wars had been raging for nine long years, ever since the Battle of Powick Bridge in 1642. The Royalist soldiers were tired, scared and holed up in a churchyard with a Parliamentarian army approaching, preparing to defend themselves. The musketeers would have checked their gunpowder and made sure they had enough musket balls. They would have loaded their guns with gunpowder and ammunition and waited, knowing that their lack of armour meant their chances of surviving the attack were slim.

The south-facing wall of Powick Church offers a clue about what else happened that day. Close to the ground, look for a couple of vertical incisions. These are where the walls of the church were used as sharpening stones, probably to sharpen the points of pikes – metal spikes attached to the end of a long ash pole that were used to spear horses used in cavalry attacks. In extremis, churches were not considered sacrosanct. During the British Civil Wars, some had the lead from their roofs stripped to make musket balls, and one even had its organ pipes melted down. If you were about to face your enemy, you would prepare in any way you could, including using the building stone to sharpen your weapon. And attacking soldiers had no compunction about damaging church buildings, either, as the musket ball dints higher up the wall show.

Of course, we don't know that it was Royalist soldiers who sharpened their pikes here; it could have been Parliamentarians, after the surviving Royalists had fled, taking a break before pushing on to the next stage of the battle. This was the Battle of Worcester, when the Royalists were finally defeated, marking the end of the wars. But all the soldiers knew at the time was that they were attacking or attacked, trying to kill and save their own lives, fighting for King and country – or just country – and preparing for the next onslaught.

ADDRESS Upton Road, Powick, WR2 4QT TIP To see the site of the first battle of the British Civil Wars, head north on the A449, cross the large roundabout, then take the first left. The bridge is on your left.

80 Forge Mill Needle Museum

Blind to the idea of health and safety at work

Workers often complain about the rigours of current health and safety regulations. A visit to the Forge Mill Needle Museum provides an excellent illustration of what life was like when health and safety risk assessments were somewhat lax.

During the Industrial Revolution, many water mills were converted to industrial use. Forge Mill was first built in 1570 and was added to and altered as required until 1958, when it closed. It was converted to needle production in 1729.

The needles were sharpened by a 'pointer' who rolled the wire against a spinning sharpening stone. This created a lot of dust, and without extraction or respiratory protection, it usually took only a couple of years before pointers started coughing up blood. Most died within 10 years. There were several other hazards associated with this work as well. Sometimes, the needle points would fly off, and pointers were identifiable by the scars on their faces, known as twitters. If they were unlucky, one of the needle points would land in an eye and blind them. Pointers were sometimes issued with Personal Protective Equipment, although we might not immediately recognise it as such: they would wear a paper hat, so if a spark that flew from the wheel landed on their head, they could quickly whip it off – an altogether better option than having a head full of burning hair. These days, sharpening stones come with a 'use-by' date to reduce the risk of their shattering. Before the introduction of health and safety regulations, pointing wheels occasionally exploded. That is what killed one of the pointers at this mill. Part of the shattered stone was inscribed with 1816, the year of Edward Mathew's death, and built into the outside wall.

So, next time you are frustrated by health and safety measures, perhaps remember those who worked, suffered and died without them.

ADDRESS Needle Mill Lane, Riverside, Redditch, B98 8HY, +44 (0) 1527 62509, www.forgemill.org.uk, info@forgemill.org.uk TIP Stepping even further back in time, the Bordesley Abbey Visitor Centre is next to the museum, with the abbey in the meadows to the north.

81 Positivity Rocks

COVID kindness

During the 2010s, an unusual movement gained momentum. People painted rocks and left them where others might find them. Sometimes, they just painted pictures, but many also added comforting words. In some areas, people were encouraged to collect the rocks. In others, they were encouraged to take a photo of any they found, post it on social media, then move the stone to another location so someone else could experience the thrill of spotting it.

In 2020, when the COVID pandemic paralysed the country and isolated many people, communities revived the habit of leaving painted rocks to support and lift the mood of strangers. Here in Redditch, Lauren Mernagh began painting supportive messages on stones that she left along her street. This small act of kindness fired the imagination of so many others that the line she started grew to 7,000 painted rocks and created a trail around the Arrow Valley Country Park. When COVID restrictions were lifted, the rocks were collected up, and 1,000 were chosen to create a lasting memorial. They have been placed together to create a rainbow – a symbol of optimism, solidarity and gratitude to frontline workers during the pandemic. In a time when the whole population was restricted from connecting in person, small actions like this gave people hope, reminded them that others cared, and brought smiles to many faces.

Stone painting is still practised, giving joy to both the painter and the finder. Stone caterpillars snake across gardens of children's hospices, painted rocks are piled in prayer, and sometimes, if you hunt hard enough, you might spot one hidden in the hollow of a tree, ready to be admired, photographed and moved to another hiding place for someone else to discover.

This memorial reminds us that, during trying times, communities can support each other and look forward to a brighter future.

ADDRESS Arrow Valley Visitor Centre, Battens Drive, Redditch, B98 0LJ TIP If you head north from the visitor centre car park, you will find the Family Art Trail, featuring sculptures of some of the wild residents of the park (www.redditchbc.gov.uk/things-to-do).

82 Bonzo's Grave

Percussion pilgrimage

Pilgrimages to churches are not uncommon, although they usually involve the relics of a saint, which are believed to offer an enhanced channel of communication with God. Here at St Michael's Church in Rushock, people conduct a different type of pilgrimage, for this is where the ashes of John 'Bonzo' Bonham are interred. It's probably fair to suggest that, as the drummer of pioneering heavy rock band Led Zeppelin, who died from choking on his own vomit after excessive drinking, Bonzo was probably not a saint.

There is little doubt, though, that he was an extremely talented drummer who pushed the boundaries of musical possibility. He was not a drummer who merely played the background beat while the other band members took the lead – his drum solo, 'Moby Dick', was a key element of live performances and often lasted over 20 minutes. For a drummer to hold the attention of an audience for that length of time is remarkable.

And that is why he is still revered by drummers and rock music aficionados almost half a century after his death. Such was his charisma and power in entrancing his audiences that admirers still make a pilgrimage to his grave and leave an offering of a cymbal or drumsticks to show their appreciation for his life.

After Bonzo's death, Led Zeppelin disbanded, but their music lives on as the records are remastered and re-released, and films of their time together as a band are also made public. The music, of which Bonzo's contribution was an integral part, continues to resonate with audiences today. For him, drumming was an art form that he had been perfecting since he was five years old. Although he lived only 32 short years, he made a significant contribution to the lives of many people and will no doubt continue to do so, inspiring more pilgrimages to this small church in rural Worcestershire, for fans to pay their respects.

ADDRESS St Michael and All Angels Church, Rushock, WR9 0NR TIP If opera is more your sort of music, you might like to visit the grave of Jenny Lind, the 'Swedish Nightingale', in Great Malvern Cemetery (Madresfield Road, WR14 2AT).

83 Shelsley Walsh Hill Climb

Speedy Specials

Imagine streaking along at twice the UK's legal speed limit. Not on a motorway, but on a road that twists and turns up a Worcestershire hillside. This is what drivers have been known to do during speed trials on the Shelsley Walsh Hill Climb.

The climb is 1,000 yards long, and its steepest gradient is 1:7. People have completed the challenge in sports cars, classic cars, estate cars, SUVs, electric cars and even tractors. Some have done away with the engine altogether; there are speed records for cycling up the climb, and even for running it.

But the challenges at Shelsley Walsh are not all about speed. The sporting trials see teams of two competing to reach the highest point of the hill on a route over grass, bracken and mud. The off-road cars used in this challenge are specially designed to turn in a small space, and the passenger moves around to distribute the weight over different wheels, depending on where more traction is needed. Reaching the top of the course is not a given.

Creativity, imagination and fun are also at play at Shelsley Walsh gatherings. Their annual Classic Nostalgia event thrums with festival vibes as well as the growl of exhaust pipes. Entertainment includes live music, vintage fashion, displays by car clubs and, of course, food. Races feature a wide range of cars, including Shelsley Specials. These are unique vehicles, individually built and designed to be as lightweight as possible within the constraints of the chassis. Bodywork is optional – every gram counts! 106 have been registered since 1920, and they can be identified by a Shelsley Special label that is applied to successful vehicles.

If you are more of a doer than a spectator, you can even have a go at the hill climb yourself. How quickly would you – and your car – make it to the top? Would you dare to reach the motorway speed limit? Or even double it?

ADDRESS Shelsley Walsh, WR6 6RP, +44 (0) 1886 812211, www.shelsleywalsh.com
TIP St Andrew's Church in Shelsley Walsh houses impressive woodwork and a rare chancel screen that the poet Sir John Betjeman described as 'the finest in the county'.

84 Cork Oak Tree

A uniquely sustainable bark harvest

Walking through the woodlands of Spain or Portugal, it can be a little confusing at first when you see trees with a smooth, reddish trunk up to the height of about six feet, with knobbly, gnarly, greyish bark above that. On closer inspection, it becomes clear that the lower sections of bark have been stripped. If you were to do this to any other species in the world, the tree would die, as it would be unable to transport sugars from its leaves back down to its roots. In fact, foresters sometimes do this intentionally to kill trees, and squirrels can do it unintentionally, causing the tree to sprout shoots below the damaged ring.

Quercus suber – the Cork Oak – is the exception that proves the rule. It is possible to harvest this tree's bark every 9 to 12 years without causing any damage to the tree at all. Cork is the ultimate sustainably produced product, resulting in wildlife-rich woodland habitats, and is totally renewable. As most Cork Oaks live for 150 to 200 years, they can usually be harvested 12 times during their lifespan and produce around 4,000 bottle corks. A specialist axe is used to remove the bark in as few as two pieces. It is left stacked to season for a year, then boiled and pressed flat, before being graded. Historically, much of the harvest was used to cork wine bottles, but with the introduction of plastic corks and metal screw caps, the industry has declined, along with the habitats it supported.

It is unlikely that you will ever see the bark harvested from the Cork Oak tree at Spetchley Park Gardens. It is a beautiful specimen tree, standing near the root house towards the southern end of the gardens, and is passed by visitors following the Pleasure Garden Walk and the Lake Walk. The gardens have many other specimen trees and features that will interest anyone who enjoys spending time in beautifully managed landscapes.

ADDRESS Spetchley Park Gardens, Spetchley, WR5 1RS, www.spetchleyparkestate.co.uk **TIP** For a walk in woods managed for wildlife and with free admission, head west to Worcester Woods Country Park.

85 Stone House Garden

A garlanded garden and nurturing nursery

Louisa Arbuthnott has a passion for plants. When she and her husband James moved to Stone House Cottage Nursery over 50 years ago, they decided on the broad structure of the walled garden together, planting yew hedges to create vistas and delineate different areas. James learned to lay bricks and added flourishes to the walls over the following years. These include several towers and gazebos, each built to different heights and styles, which lend a romantic dimension to the garden.

But the walls are not all about romance. Each one soaks up and radiates heat, casts shade, and offers shelter differently, depending on its angle and its relationship to other structures around it. This means the walls, aided by the hedges, have created a plethora of microclimates, all in the same garden. They also offer structures up which climbers can be trained.

This is where Louisa's passion comes into play. With her eye for combining colour, texture and form, plus her knowledge of plants, she has spent the last 50 years playing here – and working incredibly hard, managing the garden and nursery on her own. She is always looking out for rare plants that she might have just created the right conditions for, taking cuttings and growing things from seed.

One wonders whether the sign that warns visitors not to take cuttings, and that suspects may be searched and shot, is only half in jest, as the income from the nursery, which sells plants grown from cuttings, pays for the garden. If you are a gardener, you will be delighted by the rare plants on offer and the opportunity to see how they grow in a real garden, with Louisa on hand to offer advice, should you want it. If you are not, make a donation and wander through the garden anyway – it is a riotous abundance of delight, mixing formal and flamboyant, flowers and form. You are bound to leave with a smile blooming across your face!

ADDRESS Church Lane, Kidderminster, DY10 4BG, www.shcn.co.uk **TIP** If spending time in a walled garden with no food has teased your tastebuds, Hogarths Stone Manor hotel's afternoon tea is very highly regarded (about half a mile SE on the A448).

86 Tardebigge Flight

The longest lock flight in Britain

For those used to travelling by car or train, it might not be evident that Birmingham sits on a raised plateau above a wide hinterland that includes Worcestershire. This becomes more obvious when travelling by canal from Birmingham to Worcester.

The first half of the 29-mile-long journey after leaving Birmingham is flat, although if you are walking it, you will have to cross the Wast Hills, where the long tunnel does not have a towpath. It is not until the canal has skirted Alvechurch that you reach the edge of the plateau and will notice things change. First, there are two tunnels, quite close together, then an exceptionally deep lock where there was initially a boat lift.

The boat lift was created as an alternative to locks; this canal was dug during the Industrial Revolution, a time of great creativity and, inevitably, engineers of the age would seek alternatives to replace old designs. Since Leonardo da Vinci created this lock design in the 15th century, it is no surprise that others have tried to update it. However, they quickly decided that boat lifts would not be sturdy enough and reverted to this centuries-old technology instead.

A reservoir was constructed to ensure that the locks did not run out of water, with a pump to raise supplies to the top of the flight. Over the next few miles, the canal descends through 30 locks, with an average drop of just over six feet per lock. The stretch of water between each, which makes it a flight rather than a staircase, also means it spans a longer distance, and the locks are not all visible at once, so this is not the most spectacular series of locks in Britain. However, it remains a finely balanced and exceedingly well-calculated marvel of engineering, and enabled the success of the canal, which was used, among other things, to carry chocolate crumb to the Cadbury factory at Bournville.

ADDRESS Tardebigge, B60 1NF to Bromsgrove, B60 3AU **TIP** The popular Queens Head pub has outdoor space and seating next to the canal, just below Tardebigge Bottom Lock (www.queensheadbromsgrove.co.uk).

87 Kyre Park Dovecote

Only for high-fliers

Britain remains a hierarchical society. However, modern Britain has nothing on the past. There were times when castles could only be built with the permission of the monarch. There were times when anyone could tell the social class of someone else by what they were wearing; in the 14th century, only those with an income of £100 per year or more were allowed to wear furs. Only lords with land worth £1,000 a year and their families were permitted to wear whatever they liked. Even knights were restricted.

And when this dovecote was built around 1600, only the Lord of the Manor or the clergy, who had been given specific permission by them, were permitted to keep pigeons or doves. Because dovecotes were such a status symbol, they were often built in conspicuous places, which is why this one once stood on the south side of the house, rather than hidden behind buildings as it now is.

Apart from conveying status, dovecotes also served a practical purpose. Young pigeons, known as squabs, were taken from their ledges and eaten before they fledged and became tough. This was an important source of meat for the lordly household. Dovecotes also provided a source of eggs, feathers and manure for gardens. The downside was that the 1,200 or so birds that lived in a dovecote like this ate a huge volume of grain and seed, often upsetting tenant farmers, as it significantly affected their income, whilst adding to the lord's food stocks.

On the outside of this dovecote, you can see a protruding ring, and if you step inside, taking care not to disturb its current peafowl residents, you will see other protruding rings all the way up the structure. This was to prevent climbing predators, such as ferrets, from reaching the nesting birds. The ladder attached to the rotating pole is known as a potence, and was designed to enable the collection of squabs and eggs from the nesting holes.

ADDRESS Kyre Park and Gardens, Tenbury Wells, WR15 8RW, www.kyrepark.com
TIP The half-timbered National Trust dovecote at Hawford is even older than this one (www.nationaltrust.org.uk).

88 Pump Rooms

Well, well, well... Tenbury's big idea

In contrast to Malvern's water, which is renowned for containing nothing at all and springing from the ground uninvited, Tenbury's water was only discovered in 1839 when one of the townsfolk sank a deeper well, hoping for a better quality drinking water supply. Until then, Tenbury was a market town, its only connection to water being the River Teme, which flows nearby. Much to his surprise, Mr Godson did not find lovely clean drinking water in his new well, but rather foul-smelling brine, rich in iodine.

An entrepreneur at heart, Mr Godson decided to join the 'spa town' trend, capitalising on the Victorian wellness craze. He built a small bathhouse, but it lost money and closed in 1855. However, with the opening of the railway in 1861, Mr Godson's interest was renewed. He commissioned James Cranston to design the Pump Rooms, completed in 1862. Cranston's design was inspired by some glasshouses he was developing at the same time, but using sheets of steel instead of glass.

'Wells' was added to Tenbury's name, and the Pump Rooms attracted visitors to the town, although perhaps not in the numbers hoped for. The rooms featured unisex bathing areas and consulting rooms for those with conditions it was thought the water would help. The octagonal part of the building with a pointed roof housed the pumps, along with a drinking fountain. It is said that the water smelled akin to recently discharged gunpowder due to its mineral content. Presumably, the taste would have been equally unpalatable. It must have taken some determination to drink it!

Having fallen into disrepair in the 20th century, the Pump Rooms have now been fully refurbished and are used as an office, meeting room and ceremonial space. Their unique design adds an unusual architectural flair to Tenbury Wells, making this market town even more appealing to visitors.

ADDRESS Teme Street, Tenbury Wells, WR15 8BA, +44 (0) 1584 810118, www.tenburytowncouncil.gov.uk/the-pump-rooms TIP Unwined Bar & Bistro on Market Street is a very popular restaurant, renowned for its award-winning tapas (www.unwinedbarandbistro.co.uk).

89 Cholera Burial Ground

A preventable pandemic

Since the 19th century, seven cholera pandemics have been recorded by the World Health Organisation, with the final one ongoing. This burial ground was used during the 1832 pandemic. The previous year, the disease was reported to be spreading through India, and it arrived on these shores in Sunderland. It travelled to Worcestershire up the River Severn. Little was known about the disease – just that once affected, people suffered from extreme vomiting and diarrhoea, turned an unhealthy bluish-grey colour and could die in a matter of hours. The treatment offered made things worse, encouraging further vomiting and diarrhoea, thus accelerating dehydration.

As it spread, towns across the country were encouraged to set up separate burial grounds for cholera victims, and this is the one for Upton. Having the burials here moved the mourners away from the crowded town, helping to control hysteria. It also relieved pressure on the already full churchyard down by the river. In this area, 37 people are listed as having died from this pandemic, including men and women, old and young. The main unifying factor was poverty.

And that continues to be the case. Although the last pandemic to affect the UK occurred in 1893, cases of the disease worldwide are believed to be increasing. We now know that cholera is spread by eating food or drinking water contaminated with the Vibrio cholerae bacteria – and that safe water, basic sanitation and good hygiene are effective in preventing the disease. We also know that it is easily treated by rehydration. And yet, despite how easy this disease is to prevent and treat, it is estimated that there are still over a million cases and thousands of deaths every year.

Park at the end of the lane that joins New Street just before the greenhouses start on the left. Walk down the lane, and the burial ground is in the field on the right.

ADDRESS New Street, west of Upton **TIP** In 2023, a picture of the signpost on the corner of New Street and High Street in Upton went viral because the sign links a children's play area with the burial ground.

90 Clive's Fruit Farm

A delicious day out

Pick Your Own farms are no longer places where you grub around in the straw on the ground, looking for berries the slugs have not found first; they have become destinations in their own right, and Clive's is an excellent example of that development. Perfect strawberries in planters hang at the perfect picking height. Raspberries remain more of a challenge, as the fruit tends to hide underneath leaves. The best way to find the lush red berries is still to bend down and look up. Developments in soft fruit varieties and growing methods, such as the use of polytunnels, mean they have a far longer season than they used to. The polytunnels also make picking your own produce an attractive proposition, even when it's raining. The farm also has sweet cherries, crunchy apples and juicy pears – and just as the fruit crops are waning, the pumpkin field comes into its own, just in time for Halloween.

If you don't have the time or the inclination to pick your own, the farm shop sells ready-picked fruit from the farm and vegetables from other local growers, fruit juice and cider pressed on the farm, and all sorts of delicacies. And although this is a fruit farm by name, the attraction that draws many visitors is the butcher's and their fabulous Scotch eggs. To turn your visit into a real occasion, there is a playground for children, an assortment of farm animals in the fields next to the car park, and a gorgeous café.

Many people who live in Worcestershire find that they have an old apple or pear tree in their garden, and each tree can produce as much as a tonne of fruit – far more than one family can consume. Clive's has a solution to this problem as well – contract juicing, allowing local residents to drink their very own professionally pressed and bottled fruit juice.

Everyone knows the value of time spent outside in nature, and a day out at Clive's can work wonders!

ADDRESS Upper Hook Road, Upton upon Severn, WR8 0SA, +44 (0) 1684 592664, www.clivesfruitfarm.co.uk, office@clivesfruitfarm.co.uk **TIP** If you are in the north of the county, or like the idea of picking your own vegetables throughout every season, check out Stanleys, near Kidderminster, as an alternative (stanleysfarmshop.co.uk).

91 George VI Letter Box

Postal progress

When the government first established a postal monopoly, it set a standard fee for delivering a letter from one point to another in the UK. In towns, a 'bellman' walked around, ringing his bell and collecting mail to take to a receiving house (a precursor to a Post Office). However, for villagers, receiving houses were often miles away, making the service difficult to access.

The author Anthony Trollope, who worked for the General Post Office, noticed that some countries had resolved this issue by placing secure boxes in strategic locations, into which people could post their letters. Before long, a trial was introduced in Jersey. It was deemed a success and rolled out across the rest of the country in 1853.

By the time George VI was crowned in the 1930s, brilliant red letter boxes were a familiar sight. Apart from its colour, what makes this one unusual is that it is made of wood rather than cast iron. This was because sub-postmasters were required to have a letter box and pay for it themselves. James Ludlow & Son spotted an opportunity and manufactured wall letter boxes from pine, with a steel plate on the outside. Because pine was cheaper than cast iron, they were popular, and over 5,000 once adorned sub-post offices and other buildings. They were not as secure as cast-iron letter boxes, so the printed enamel plate warned against using them to post valuable items.

Not all letter boxes are red. Exceptions include a few blue airmail boxes from the 1930s, more blue boxes painted as a tribute to NHS workers during the COVID-19 pandemic, and gold ones to celebrate local gold medal winners at the 2012 London Olympics. This one was repainted after being decommissioned when the Post Office moved. It is one of only a few hundred of this style left in Britain, so it is fortunate that the Post Office listened to local people's wishes to maintain the box.

ADDRESS 16 Old Street, Upton upon Severn, WR8 0HA **TIP** There are four red cast-iron letter boxes in Malvern that are listed because of their unique design. You can find one of them at the corner of St Andrew's Road and Peachfield Road.

92 Ham Meadow

Baked-in biodiversity

Upton is best known for three things: music festivals, its unusual density of pubs, and flooding after heavy rainfall further up the river's catchment. Walk along the riverside path, and you will notice the flood barrier protecting the town, as the rising waters of the River Severn used to frequently deluge it, causing significant damage. However, one part of Upton has benefited from the floods for a long time: Ham Meadow.

Continue heading south past the end of the flood barriers, and it does not take long to reach the Upton Ham Nature Reserve. When the river floods this area, the water slows down and deposits silt across the meadow. That silt can be disastrous for crops, so the area has never been 'improved' for agriculture, but it provides perfect conditions for a wide range of wildflowers. This is a Lammas meadow, which means several families have historically owned it, but it has been left unfenced. From February, the grass and wildflowers were left to grow, and in July, each family cut the hay from their portion of the land using scythes. From Lammas Day, a Christian festival on 1 August that celebrates the harvest with a loaf of bread made from the new season's wheat, the area is grazed as common land for the rest of the year.

This regime of flooding, cutting, munching and manuring has continued for hundreds of years and created a meadow rich in wildflowers, including the vivid purple meadow crane's-bill and the pale pink common bistort. In turn, these attract insects and butterflies, such as Common Blues, Gatekeepers and Meadow Browns. The site also supports a wide variety of birds, including waders such as redshanks and curlews, and ground-nesting birds such as skylarks and corn buntings. June is the best time to visit, but please stick to the paths and keep dogs on a short lead to avoid trampling birds' eggs.

ADDRESS South of Dunn's Lane, Upton upon Severn, WR8 0JD TIP Asham Meadow is another Lammas meadow, which is flooded by the River Avon near Birlingham (www.kemerton.org).

93 Aqua Park Assault Course

A watery adventure

What do you call a cross between a bouncy castle and an obstacle course, floating on water? It sounds like the basis of a joke, but it is not, although a visit to Aztec Adventure aqua park will almost certainly make you laugh.

This inflatable obstacle course is open from May to September. This is not the Caribbean – even in summer, the water will be cold, but on a hot day, that first icy trickle down the neck of your wetsuit might offer a welcome respite from the heat. On a cool day, it might be a bit of a shock – but you won't stay cold for long as you slither, slide and splash around the course. For the best part of an hour, your heart will pound with excitement and exertion. Perhaps you will challenge yourself to stay out of the water as you run from obstacle to obstacle and leap between them. Perhaps you will even be successful for a short while, although you are unlikely to stay dry for long. Or perhaps you will just lark around, leaping and laughing, welcoming the wobble and splash of this watery adventure.

Here, you can embrace the energy of others, too. Enjoy the spectacle of a teenager showing off to their friends, weaving around the course, looking invincible – until they realise they are not… falling with a look of surprise, and surfacing with a look of delight. As 12-year-old clambers up a tower ahead of you as though gravity didn't exist, will you unexpectedly find yourself racing to prove you can do it, too?

Even on a grey day, a visit to the aqua park will brighten your summer. There are towers to climb, slides to zip down, bars to balance on and trampolines to bounce on. This is not the place to go for a lazy summer's day, unless you choose to sit on the banks and watch your friends and family having fun. Which is, of course, an option for those who don't want to feel that initial icy finger of water sliding down their back.

ADDRESS Aztec Adventure, Worcester Road, Upton Warren, B61 7ER, www.aztecadventure.co.uk/activities/aqua-park **TIP** For a somewhat drier adventure, the Riverside Gardens at Webbs, just over the A48, are a series of display gardens designed by a Chelsea Flower Show gold medal winner. They are free to enter (www.webbsdirect.co.uk/wychbold).

94 Brewers Arms

Community owned since 2022

As the value of houses in England grew through the 1980s into the noughties, the temptation to sell village pubs and turn them into housing was more than many could resist; the financial gains to be made from selling to a property developer were far greater than those to be made from running a pub in a small village. The government recognised this issue and addressed it in the 2011 Localism Act. This provided a structure through which a community could nominate an asset, such as a local pub, as an 'asset of community value'. If it meets the requirements, it becomes protected. An asset of community value cannot be sold without giving the community an opportunity to raise the funds needed to buy it.

In West Malvern, the Lamb Inn closed in 2013, leaving only one pub in the village. The Brewers Arms is small and relatively inaccessible, and the owner found it hard to make it commercially viable, so local people set up and invested in a Community Benefit Society, which bought the pub in 2022. They renovated it and found a tenant who now runs the pub and kitchen, with the help of villagers who volunteer their time.

The Brewers Arms is ideal for those walking or cycling on the hills, and popular with locals catching up with their friends and neighbours. The garden has incredible views across Herefordshire to Wales, and in winter, the cosy bar has a roaring log fire. The building in the garden, known as the Armpit, is used by community groups and those with something to celebrate, and it also offers extra seating in the warmer months. The pub serves superb food, and its popularity means that, as there are no reservations, it is a good idea to arrive as early as possible. Please note: the pub does not have a car park, or even a tarmacked road leading to it. There is a small parking area nearby on West Malvern Road – or you could always walk or cycle.

ADDRESS Lower Dingle, West Malvern, WR14 4BQ, www.brewersarmswestmalvern.co.uk
TIP Another popular pub nearby with excellent views over Herefordshire from the garden is The Chase Inn (www.thechaseinnmalvern.co.uk).

95 Pear Tree Cottage Garden

Wisteria hysteria

If you had a beautiful garden wrapped around your house with views over the surrounding countryside, what would you do with it? Sit and enjoy the panorama with a glass of gin and tonic? Swing in a hammock and enjoy the view up through the branches of the trees? The owners of Pear Tree Cottage Garden have undoubtedly done those things, but they did not stop there. Instead of relaxing in their garden, they decided to open it to the public to raise money for the National Garden Scheme. This is not a relaxing pursuit, making sure the garden looks perfect for each open day and visiting group. But the hard work has been hugely rewarding. Not only does this garden give immense joy to every visitor, but it has also raised tens of thousands of pounds for medical charities.

The National Garden Scheme (also known as the Yellow Book) gives garden lovers the chance to nose around other people's private gardens, and often to eat cake, too, paying a small fee for the privilege. In doing so, it has become the largest donor to nursing charities in the UK, giving millions of pounds each year.

Pear Tree Cottage Garden is known for its 'Wisteria Hysteria' events each May, when the front of the house is draped in cascades of lilac flowers. But the garden continues to perform throughout the season. It is the glittering details, freshly curated each year, that set it apart from other gardens: a tree with a gin tap, the world's smallest potting shed, rare plants, hidden seats, sculptures dotted around. This garden is full of love: love for plants, people, the view, gardening, family and sharing. It is no wonder that Pear Tree Cottage Garden continues to draw visitors and improve the lives of so many through the National Garden Scheme charity. For that, we have the family to thank – for working hard to share their garden, rather than simply relaxing in it themselves.

ADDRESS Witton Hill, Wichenford, WR6 6YX, www.ngs.org.uk/gardens/pear-tree-cottage-wr6 **TIP** As well as NGS gardens, many villages in Worcestershire hold open garden events. Fladbury Walkabout combines open gardens with a flower festival, live music and other activities (www.fladburywalkabout.com).

96 Wolverley Pound

A cool enclosure

Most villages would have had a pound at some point, to hold stray livestock; the owner paid a ransom to cover the cost of care before the animals were released. Although many villages had a pound in the Middle Ages, Wolverley's is thought to be more modern, from the early 19th century. This may well be as a result of the Wolverley Enclosure Act, which was passed in 1775. The Enclosure Acts were Acts of Parliament whereby common land, farmed by local people without fencing, was given a stock-proof boundary and taken into private ownership, usually by someone in a higher social class. These newly enclosed fields were often used for grazing livestock, as the landowners saw this as a more profitable enterprise than the villagers growing food for themselves. Until the Wolverley Enclosure Act was passed, it seems unlikely that many people would be concerned about stray animals, as all the land was held in common.

Many pounds were created by building walls or simply erecting a fenced enclosure with a gate. One of the reasons Wolverley Pound is so special is also why it has lasted so long: this pound has been carved into the local bedrock, which is soft sandstone. This made the pound more secure than a fenced enclosure, and of course, it has lasted longer.

In this area, the underlying geology means there are several rock dwellings and caves carved into sandstone nearby. Rock dwellings might seem very basic to us these days, but they provide a good level of shelter and an even temperature to their inhabitants. Some of the local caves have been used by pubs in the past to provide additional seating for their customers, but because they are popular with bats, which are protected, they are no longer open to the public. So, Wolverley Pound is possibly the best place in the immediate area to get a feel for what a rock dwelling might have been like.

ADDRESS Wolverley Road, Wolverley, DY11 5XA TIP If you head just over the border into Staffordshire, the National Trust has some rock houses you can explore inside on Kinver Edge (www.nationaltrust.org.uk).

97 The Boardroom

Where history was made

Charles Hastings was such a gifted medical student that when he graduated in the early 19th century, people expected him to head to the bright lights of London to pursue his career. However, having grown up in Martley, he wanted to serve his home county and instead practised at Worcester Medical Infirmary (which did not receive 'Royal' status until the 20th century). Receiving treatment here depended on finding a hospital sponsor who had not yet reached the full patient allocation for the size of their donation. This left many working-class people without access to hospital care. Rather than just treating the patients he saw, Hastings considered the root causes of some of the city's prevalent health issues. For example, crowded housing with insufficient sanitation increased the risk of the spread of disease, so he invested some of his own money in new housing with better conditions, and the city's death rate dropped considerably.

Along the same lines, Hastings realised that it was a good idea for doctors to share knowledge to improve their understanding of medical issues, rather than just relying on personal experience. To this end, in 1832 he was instrumental in founding the Provincial Medical and Surgical Association, which, having extended its membership to include London doctors, later became the British Medical Association. Although the BMA now principally acts as the UK's main doctors' union, in its early years it was set up to share knowledge, research diseases and medical matters, and set standards for the profession. It was instrumental in the establishment of the General Medical Council, which regulates the profession and sets qualification standards. And the inaugural meeting of the association was held right here, in this boardroom, in what is now fittingly known as the Charles Hastings Building.

ADDRESS Infirmary Museum, Charles Hastings Building, Castle Street, Worcester, WR1 3AS, www.medicalmuseum.org.uk TIP The boardroom is in one of two medical museums in Worcester. The other is at Worcester Royal Infirmary and shows how healthcare has changed over the last 300 years (www.medicalmuseum.org.uk/georgemarshallmuseum).

98 The Buzz

Bouncy castles for big kids

Have you ever seen a colourful bouncy castle at an event, thought it looked like fun, headed over and slipped your shoes off, only to then realise with a sinking heart that adults were forbidden to play on it? If so, this bee-themed bouncing bonanza is for you – and it is so much more than a single castle! Anyone, of any age, can bounce, run, leap and slide to their heart's content at The Buzz. Will you float over the obstacles like a butterfly, or be stung by one of them like a bee? Will teamwork help you and your friends get around the circuit faster? Or will you see whether you can beat the course time record, running solo against the clock?

This indoor inflatable adventure has towers to climb, tunnels to squeeze through, pillars to weave between, slides to slip down and obstacles to navigate. It's guaranteed to make you laugh as you bounce in an unanticipated direction, careen off the walls and bump into unexpected protrusions. Unless you are ultra-fit, it's also guaranteed to remind you that you are not as athletic as you thought, as you try to run while bouncing and laughing, not quite fully in control of your movements.

This is the perfect place for a stag do or hen party (although it might be best to abandon any veils, tiaras or mankinis for the duration), a team-building event, or just a jolly with friends or family. There are adult-only sessions where everyone is over 16, or you can book the whole place for yourselves.

And if you do have young people in your party, it's never too early to start the bouncing fun. Why not take generations of the family with you? The children will get a buzz from it just as much as the adults. And, if anyone does not quite feel up to the boisterous nature of the activity, they can always retire to the café and watch all the action on the big screens while relaxing with a coffee instead.

ADDRESS The Old Railway Yard, Midland Road, Worcester, WR5 1DS, www.thebuzzworcester.co.uk TIP If bouncing around for an hour has not worn you out, you could also have a go on the climbing wall next door (www.redpointworcester.co.uk).

99 Community Garden

Buzzing with life

The buzz of the racecourse in Worcester extends beyond dressing up, assessing the fitness of horses and jockeys, the thrill of a bet and the reverberation of hooves pounding the ground as the horses thunder past. Head to the northern end of the racecourse, and the buzz of insects adds another dimension to the experience. Here, you will find Worcester Community Garden, where visitors are welcome to wander and contemplate life, or roll up their sleeves and help out.

On an old concrete stable yard, volunteers have created a series of small gardens, all humming with life. The pollinator garden is full of attractive plants, with insect hotels and beehives to provide shelter – the former above likely flood height, the latter on a floating pontoon, as the site is often inundated with water. It is not only the horses that move fast around here, especially when heavy rain is forecast. As the river rises, so the flood defence team races around the site, securing items that might be washed away and preparing the floating office, polytunnel, composting toilet and beehives so they rise with the water.

The vertical garden and balcony, showcasing how easy it is to grow a beautiful edible garden in a tiny space, escape the challenges of flooding by being raised from the ground by design. Some of the fruit trees are planted on ridges, so their roots are submerged for less time as floodwaters recede. The allotment garden must additionally be protected from badgers, who show considerable determination and ingenuity when it comes to reaching their favourite vegetables.

Other gardens offer more inspiration for aspiring gardeners, cut flowers for purchase, colour and wildlife, and the opportunity to commune with nature and get dirt under your fingernails – it's not just the bees around here that are buzzing, but the volunteers and visitors, too.

ADDRESS Pitchcroft Racecourse, Worcester, WR1 3JW, www.worcestercommunitygarden.org.uk, admin@worcestercommunitygarden.org.uk
TIP If your visit to the community garden has inspired you to flex your green fingers, St Peters Garden Centre is popular for its plants and café. Find it just to the south of Worcester (www.stpetersgardencentre.co.uk).

100 Diglis Fish Pass

Cascading success

Until the middle of the 19th century, the River Severn at Worcester was aptly named: it was only navigable for up to seven months of the year. For the other five months, the transportation of goods such as gloves, porcelain and Worcestershire Sauce was far more challenging. To resolve this issue, four new locks and weirs were constructed to maintain the water level.

Unfortunately, a weir not only stops water from moving along the river – it also stops fish. Although salmon could leap the weir, smaller, weaker fish such as twaite shad could not. From hundreds of thousands swimming up the river to spawn, the twaite shad became one of the UK's rarest fish. Unlocking the Severn, a multi-agency collaboration, was set up to turn back the tide. Four fish passes were built on the River Severn, and two weirs were modified on the Teme. Many fish passes are designed for salmon or trout, both natural leapers, but these were configured with each rise a swimmable eight inches and pools in between to enable shad to swim up them. After the passes were built, shad were seen to have negotiated all of them, once again finding their historic spawning grounds higher up the river. The addition of spawning fish to the river provides food for insects, and the insects and young fish then become prey for other wildlife, creating a positive cascading effect on biodiversity.

At 110 yards long, 9 yards wide and 5.5 yards deep, the fish pass at Diglis was the biggest deep vertical slot fish pass in England and Wales when it was constructed, and it has a unique feature – a visitor centre with an underwater viewing window. To watch shad swimming upstream, it is best to visit during one of the drop-in sessions in May. However, the viewing gallery drop-in sessions run from March to October, and to date, 27 species of fish have been recorded heading upstream here, including eel and lamprey.

ADDRESS Diglis Dock Road, Worcester, WR5 3BS (cross the river on the footbridge and head upstream), www.canalrivertrust.org.uk/things-to-do/museums-and-attractions/diglis-island-and-fish-pass **TIP** Worcester city centre is a pleasant walk from the fish pass – just head upstream for about a mile, on either side of the river.

101 Diglis Portrait Bench

Rusty relics

One of a series of portrait benches installed on cycling routes across England, these four characters were chosen by public vote. The Roundhead (Parliamentarian) with his pike and the Cavalier (Royalist) with his gun represent the city's importance as the place where the British Civil Wars began and ended. The city was staunchly Royalist, so the Roundhead is presumably there as a nod to the victors, although the Royalists had the last laugh when the monarchy was restored.

Sir Charles Hastings, looking every bit the gentleman, resting on his cane, was responsible for founding the organisation here in Worcester that was to become the British Medical Association. The BMA was instrumental in the introduction of legislation to protect the public from unqualified doctors, and it now acts as the profession's trade union. Charles Hastings was also responsible for building new, more sanitary housing to replace some of the city's slums, thus improving public health in the city. The final figure is Ernie Payne, also known as the 'Worcester Wonder', who was on the gold medal-winning pursuit team at the 1908 Olympics.

What these portraits do not reference are any of the female high achievers connected to the city. Aethelflaed, Lady of Mercia (ruler) in the 10th century, fortified Worcester to defend it against Viking invaders. Vesta Tilley, born in Worcester in 1864, went on to become one of the most highly paid music hall performers, forging her own path and challenging gender norms as a male impersonator. Sheila Scott, who was also born in the city, learned to fly in her thirties and held over 100 world records for her long-distance solo flights in the 1950s and '60s.

Perhaps one day, public art will reflect the population as a whole. In the meantime, these steel portraits can remind us of the past – a past of historic attitudes as well as achievements.

ADDRESS Worcester, WR2 4AY TIP Sheila Scott was a student at the Alice Ottley School, which was merged into the Royal Grammar School. A blue plaque on one of the school gateposts on Upper Tything (WR1 1HP) commemorates her achievements.

102 Flood Markers

A record of remarkable river levels

Whenever significant events happen, whether calamitous or joyous, humans like to mark the occasion. And this is what has happened in Worcester with flooding. It is a frequent occurrence in the city, inevitable on low-lying land around the country's most voluminous river, so it is only the remarkable floods that are recorded on the wall by the cathedral's water gate. The three highest recorded were in 1886, 1947 and, highest of all, 1770, when the river rose rapidly to over 15 feet above summer levels. All floods since then have been compared to the Great Flood of 1770.

There are not many records relating to the 1770 flood, although we know it destroyed the church at Tenbury Wells. The 1886 flood was unusual because it occurred in summer. It rained heavily for two days and, with the ground already saturated, the rain became even heavier for the next two. The rise in river level was extraordinary – around 10 feet in one night alone. Many homes and businesses were flooded, with one silver lining: there is a report of at least one person catching their dinner in their front room!

The Great Flood of 1947 was caused by an exceptionally cold February, during which snow frequently fell but did not melt. In early March, storms arrived, bringing a rapid thaw and equally exceptional rainfall. Only a couple of years after the end of the war, newspaper reports at the time describe the aftermath as similar to that following an air raid, with roof tiles and chimney pots strewn across the ground. Locals willingly performed their civic duty, clearing trees that had blocked the roads and taking the wood home for their hearths – a service that is enthusiastically embraced in Worcestershire to this day. And dinner was again found in odd places: buckets of lamprey were collected from the electricity power station and sold for two a penny.

ADDRESS On the river side of Worcester Cathedral's Water Gate, WR1 2LH
TIP The water gate, right next to the markers, was used as a small dock for the cathedral when the river was still tidal, accessible twice a day at high water.

103 Fort Royal

Winning the battle, losing the war?

On 3 September 1651, the Battle of Worcester marked the end of the British Civil Wars, during which Parliamentarians fought to overthrow the monarchy. Two years previously, King Charles I had been executed, and Britain had become a republic. But Royalists fought on. Charles Stuart, son of King Charles I, who had been crowned King of Scotland but not England, was heading south towards London with his army to claim the crown, when his progress stalled at Worcester.

He stood on the tower of Worcester Cathedral and watched the Battle of Worcester play out around him. After several hours, he led an attack to the west of Fort Royal, but the Royalists were defeated and had to retreat. Oliver Cromwell, leader of the Parliamentarians, saw his opportunity and decided to storm Fort Royal. The attackers should not have stood a chance against a heavily defended, fortified position on the top of a hill. Nevertheless, the Parliamentarians successfully routed the Royalists, who retreated once again, this time towards the city, with their own cannons at Fort Royal firing down on them. The Royalists had lost the battle – and, it seemed, the war. Charles Stuart fled the city to live in exile, and 7,000 Royalists were imprisoned and then deported to the American colonies.

It is said that over 1,000 Royalists died that day, and only 200 Parliamentarians. But history is written by the victors, so who knows the truth behind the numbers? And who were the victors, anyway? It seems that the Parliamentarians won the Civil Wars, as Britain emerged as a republic, ruled by Parliament rather than a monarch. But it only stayed that way for a few years – on Oliver Cromwell's death, exactly seven years after the Battle of Worcester, the monarchy was restored and Charles Stuart was crowned King Charles II – and Britain remains a monarchy to this day. All those lives lost, and to what end?

ADDRESS Wyld's Lane, opposite the Commandery Road Car Park, Worcester, WR5 2LS, www.worcester.gov.uk **TIP** Use the pedestrian bridge to cross the river at Diglis and head south to visit another key battlefield, where Cromwell unexpectedly bridged the two rivers with his troops to outflank the Royalist defences at Powick Bridge.

104 Glover's Needle

Pointing to the past

At a time when transporting goods was easier by water than by road, Worcester was ideally placed on the River Severn to become a manufacturing centre. By the 15th century, a glove-making industry was well established in the city.

The glovers were a canny bunch; they formed the Worcester Guild of Glovers and persuaded Parliament to make the importation of gloves into Britain illegal. This protected their jobs from foreign competition, and while gloves were essential clothing for certain echelons of society, the industry thrived, reaching its peak around the turn of the 19th century. By then, 150 glove manufacturers in Worcester and its surrounding villages employed over 30,000 people, and almost half of all British gloves were made here. Generations of the same family worked in the trade. A seven-year apprenticeship was required for males to become cutters, learning to make the most of every hide. For every male cutter, 12 to 15 women were employed, often doing piecework at home, sewing the finished product.

However, nothing lasts forever. In 1826, the ban on imports was lifted, introducing foreign competition. It is said that many in Worcester starved as a result, and many moved to other urban areas in search of work. Almost a century later, World War I brought significant social changes, and fashion became less restrained. World War II brought even more changes, and afterwards, casual dress continued to rise in popularity. Gloves soon came to be associated with old-fashioned values rather than modernity, and the industry died.

Although officially the spire of what was St Andrew's Church, the name of Glover's Needle has stuck, reminding us of this important part of Worcester's history. At 245 feet high, it is easily the tallest construction in the city, and appears taller because it is so slender – almost like a glover's needle. Which is, of course, how it got its name.

ADDRESS Deansway, Worcester, WR1 2JD TIP If you head down to the riverside on a hot summer's day, the fountains in the paving will help to cool you down.

105 The Hive

A sweet collaboration

For town and gown to share a library might seem obvious, but it is rare: The Hive is Britain's first combined university and public library. The site between the city centre and the university campus was chosen to bring people together from both directions, and it houses the shared library, county archives and record office, a local history centre and the county's archaeology service.

The building was designed to achieve ambitious sustainability goals. Outside, a rain garden offers some protection against flooding, and diverse planting attracts wildlife, but it is the structure that is truly remarkable.

The Hive's unusual roofline allows cool air to be drawn up and extracted through the roof on hot summer days. When this is not enough to keep the building cool, river water is passed through a heat exchanger so cold water can be pumped through the structure at night. In winter, it is heated with biomass boilers. The roof collects rainwater, which is used to flush toilets and wash archaeological specimens. The building is constructed from cross-laminated wood rather than carbon-intensive steel or concrete, saving 2,000 tonnes of carbon emissions in construction. Since the library opened in 2012, the sustainability metrics have been actively monitored and managed, resulting in a building that uses only a quarter of the energy of many of its contemporaries.

The honey-coloured cladding made of copper-alloy shingles gives The Hive its honeycomb appearance. That was one reason for the name, but it was also chosen to represent how it was hoped the building would be used – for purposeful activity and to build a sense of community. And that is exactly what has happened since it was opened. Used by a diverse range of individuals and groups, for a diverse range of activities, including meetings, theatre – and even reading – The Hive has lived up to its name.

ADDRESS Sawmill Walk, The Butts, Worcester, WR1 3PD, www.thehiveworcester.org
TIP Less than 220 yards to the north, the university has renovated a much-loved building to create The Art House studios, workshops and galleries, another shared space for students and the community.

106 Masonic Museum

A secret society or a social good?

On entering Worcestershire's Masonic Library and Museum, you might be greeted with the phrase, 'The only secret we have is that we have no secrets'. Freemasonry has long been considered by many to be a secretive society that is only open to men and looks after its own, causing concerns over maintaining the patriarchal status quo and potential conflicts of interest in public life. This perception is reinforced when organisations such as the Metropolitan Police require employees to declare their Freemason membership to improve trust.

For those curious about the organisation, one way to learn more is to visit this Masonic Library and Museum. As members of the organisation, the volunteers who run it are bound to be biased towards its positive aspects, but they also have a lot of knowledge they are willing to share. They will tell you of the millions the Masons raise for charitable causes, of the fun and fraternity they benefit from, and of how there are female-only Masonic lodges in the same way there are male-only lodges.

Here, you can learn something of the organisation's symbolism, step inside an active temple, and admire the dedication to craft and cause in the creation of aprons and other Masonic curiosities. You can admire the handiwork of French Masons who, as prisoners of war in the Napoleonic Wars, crafted jewels full of Masonic symbolism; or the double-handled chamber pots that were once passed around under the table at long meetings for those who had to attend to a call of nature. You can see 400-year-old manuscripts and learn about historic Masons and their achievements during that period, including Mozart, Robert Burns, George Washington, Oscar Wilde, Winston Churchill and Peter Sellers.

For a deeper dive, the reference library contains 2,000 books, and the lending library allows you to learn more in the comfort of your home.

ADDRESS Masonic Centre, Rainbow Hill, Worcester, WR3 8LX, www.worcestermasonicmuseum.co.uk TIP In contrast to the largely male membership of the Masons, the Women's Institutes are all female. There are several in Worcester, including the Worcester Belles, who meet in St Mary's Hall, WR1 1NS (worcesterbelleswi.wixsite.com/belles).

107 Method Roastery

No-compromise coffee

Method, importing beans and roasting them here in Worcester, has long been a popular coffee brand among locals. Now there is a coffee shop, which, for many, is a favourite place to hang out with friends or take a relaxing break from work. Quality has always been of the utmost importance to the small Method team, and this ethos extends to their supply chain as well as taste.

They view the supply of coffee as an opportunity to make a positive difference in the lives of the growers and their communities. Method prefers to have long-term relationships with suppliers rather than treating the purchase of coffee as nothing more than a transaction. Enquire about the provenance of each roast, and the team can tell you which country it was grown in, which small estate, farmer or cooperative it was sourced from within that country, and what those people are doing to create lasting benefits in their community. These could include practices such as empowering women, using regenerative farming methods, growing coffee under a canopy of native trees, providing training to growers to make their businesses more efficient, or offering social housing for disadvantaged groups. Method cares about the environment, too: all their coffee is sold in compostable, plastic-free packaging.

Although best known for their coffee, the team's obsession with quality extends to their other offerings. If you are a tea drinker, you will not be disappointed. The tea here is beautifully presented, delicious and sourced with similar ethical considerations in mind. The food is equally good, and the team is friendly and knowledgeable.

Not only that, but the roasting equipment is all in view at the back of the café; you can watch the roasting while sipping the final result of this no-compromise process to create the best quality cup of coffee for the discerning coffee drinker.

ADDRESS Arches 50/51, Cherry Tree Walk, Worcester, WR1 3BH, www.methodroastery.com TIP If you fancy something more exotic to eat, continue down Cherry Tree Walk to the popular Maneki Ramen in Arch 45.

108 The Painted Chamber

Highway to heaven

In 1935, a decorator working for the Littleburys, who lived in one wing of The Commandery and ran a printworks from the other, discovered something unexpected. Underneath a layer of whitewash, he spotted some colour. On closer inspection, the family realised that the room was covered with murals. Rather than simply decorating over them, they brought in a conservator to recover what they could of the Painted Chamber and protect it for future generations.

The paintings date from 1475, when the building was still being used for its original purpose: a hospital for the sick. In those days, hospitals were run by religious orders, and prayer was considered essential to both physical health and spiritual wellbeing. It seems this room was where patients were brought to offer prayers for healing and forgiveness. The patients would have understood the meaning of the characters on the walls: saints to intercede on their behalf, each specialising in a different ailment, the archangel Michael weighing a human soul on his scales, and St Peter holding the gates to heaven. The image of God himself is reserved for the ceiling, where patients on their deathbeds would be able to see him.

The murals survived for 65 years. After that, Henry VIII dissolved the monasteries, and these Catholic images were whitewashed over, remaining hidden for almost 400 years. Ironically, the whitewash, which was designed to cover them up, actually protected them for all that time.

In the intervening period, the building was used as a family home, as one of the Royalist headquarters during the British Civil Wars, and as a college for the blind sons of gentlemen. The printworks operated from it for almost 100 years before the building was bought by the council and turned into a museum, making the paintings – and the rest of this historic building – accessible to the public.

ADDRESS The Commandery, Sidbury, Worcester, WR1 2HU, www.museumsworcestershire.org.uk **TIP** King Charles II visited The Commandery for the final battle of the British Civil Wars. King Charles House on New Street, which he used on his escape from the city, is now a popular pub (www.thekingcharleshouse.co.uk).

109 Swan Sanctuary

Angling for change

Back in the 1980s, swans across Britain were in trouble. Anglers used lead weights that sometimes became snagged and lost, and swans would ingest them, along with the weed they feed on. When most of the swans on the river in Worcester had disappeared, the council took action. They stopped issuing fishing permits and started feeding the remaining swans every day. Although this is not a natural place for swans to congregate because the river is silty and prone to flooding, those in the sanctuary are now numerous and well-loved.

The issue was the lead, which is a highly toxic substance. Chronic exposure causes fertility issues, adverse birth outcomes, high blood pressure, kidney damage, anaemia and cancer in humans. People who work in lead refineries are closely monitored to ensure that lead levels in their blood do not exceed safe thresholds. Lead has been removed from paint, petrol and pipes. And, although anglers have not been able to use lead weights since the 1980s, it is still used for ammunition – 7,000 tonnes of it is shot outdoors in the UK every year, and much of that lands on the ground. Tiny shot pellets look like grit or seeds to swans, who happily eat them, without understanding the effect on their health.

Between 50,000 and 100,000 waterbirds in the UK are thought to die from lead exposure each year, having ingested these tiny balls of poison. And it is not only waterbirds that are affected: the dead birds and the lead they contain are eaten by other scavengers, perpetuating the cascade of poisoning through the food chain.

In 2025, the government announced a ban on the use of lead shot, to take effect from the late 2020s. Let's hope it has as positive an impact as those actions taken to provide sanctuary to swans in this stretch of the river, helping the swan population to recover and thrive across the country, as it has done here.

ADDRESS Worcester Bridge, Worcester, WR2 4RL TIP On the other (east) side of the river, there is a row of benches that are ideally placed to relax on while watching the swans' antics.

110 Wyre Piddle Hoard

Thank goodness for democracy and decimalisation!

The Wars of the Roses, a conflict between the Houses of York and Lancaster for control of the English throne, raged across the country for over 30 years in the 15th century. In the midst of all that turmoil, someone in Wyre Piddle felt it prudent to bury their savings to keep them safe. We will never know who it was, why they were particularly concerned or why they did not return to retrieve the jug of coins they had buried. Maybe they were caught up in the fighting, or perhaps they tried to retrieve their hoard but couldn't find it.

Whatever the reason, the coins remained in their jug, buried in the ground undisturbed, for 500 years. They were minted during the reigns of Edward I to Edward IV (1272–1470), and amounted to... Exactly how much did they amount to? There were 219 coins altogether. If you ignore the fact that some were forgeries, you should be able to work out the total value. There were 135 groats, 39 half-groats and 45 pennies. This was 500 years before decimalisation, so it helps to know that a groat was worth 4d (old pennies). Therefore, this amounts to 663d. £6.63, right? Wrong! There were 12d in a shilling and 20 shillings in a pound, so therefore 240d in a pound. So, £2.76 in total. Only, that is not £2 and 76 pennies – it would have been £2 and something akin to 180d, or 90 half-groats, or 45 groats. Do you feel your brain overheating yet? A short four years after the hoard was unearthed and a somewhat longer five centuries after the coins were buried, the powers that be saw sense and realised that counting in multiples of 10 was a good idea for people with 10 fingers. Thank goodness for decimalisation!

Thank goodness, too, for democracy. It might sometimes seem like a bun fight in Parliament, but at least the fight stays in Parliament and has not spilled over into a civil war for a few hundred years.

ADDRESS Wyre Piddle, Pershore, WR10 2JB **TIP** If you are interested in local history, then you might like to visit Pershore Heritage Centre in the Town Hall (www.pershoreheritage.org).

111 Transport Museum

Back to the future

In the early 20th century, buses powered by internal combustion engines began to replace other forms of public transportation. However, they were not suited to every purpose, especially journeys with frequent stops. This meant that, despite the new technology, horse-drawn delivery vehicles remained in use for some time.

An alternative arose with the development of electric vehicles. The engines used no fuel while they were stationary, and from the 1930s, fleets of electric milk floats and bread vans became commonplace in Britain's residential areas. The Midlands helped to blaze this trail, producing many of those vehicles and creating demand for them. At one point, Midland Counties Dairy had 1,000 electric milk floats.

The growth in car ownership and the introduction of supermarkets largely put an end to home deliveries of milk and groceries by the 1980s. Who would have thought that in the 21st century, online retail would once again lead to a proliferation of home delivery, and that air pollution from vehicles would drive another phase of the development of electric alternatives? As the wheels on the bus go round and round, so does history.

The Transport Museum Wythall has a unique collection of milk floats and other electric delivery vehicles. Looking at them, you might understand why the British public has been relatively slow to embrace the idea of electric cars – sleek and stylish they are not! The museum is also home to the biggest collection of Midland Red buses. This bus company was the biggest in England outside London and designed and built its own buses for almost 50 years. One of their marketing posters claimed that they transported more than a million customers every day!

After many iterations, the museum is now a modern exhibition space with a miniature railway, café, bus company art gallery and a selection of other transport curiosities.

ADDRESS Chapel Lane, Wythall, B47 6JA, +44 (0) 564 826471, www.wythall.org.uk **TIP** Over the summer months, Wheels on Wednesday allows motoring enthusiasts to meet in several places in Worcestershire to showcase all sorts of vehicles (www.wheelsonwednesday.co.uk).

1
Doddington
Cleobury Mortimer
Upper Arley
Cookley
Wolverley
Foxholes
Kidderminster
Bewdley
Spennells
Bayton
Callow Hill
Milson
Mamble
Heightington
Wilden
Stourport-on-Severn
Hartlebury
Boraston
Newnham Bridge
Lindridge
Eardiston
The Common Abberley
Astley
Tenbury Wells
Severn
Great Witley
Shrawley
Little Witley
Upper Sapey
Holt Heath
Ombersley
Bockleton
Clifton upon Teme
Wichenford
Hawford
Martley
Tedstone Wafre
Claines
Hallow
Bredenbury
Knightwick
Broadwas
WORCESTER
Bromyard
Cotheridge
Alfrick
Leigh
Pencombe
Powick
Suckley
Longley Green
Callow End
Stoke Lacy
Storridge
Newland
Kempsey
Bishop's Frome
Much Cowarne
Malvern
Fromes Hill
Mathon
Guarlford
Malvern Wells
Severn Stoke
Bosbury
Yarkhill
Ashperton
Colwall
Tarrington
Wellington Heath
Welland
Upton-upon-Severn
Ledbury
Eastnor
Castlemorton
Little Marcle
Hollybush
Longdon
M50
N
0
2.1 mi
39 96 41 40 2 3 85 14 35 88 31 74 87 83 95 3 100 101 43 4 78 1 79 42 65 51 4 94 69 57 72 34 73 48 90 89 91 92 49 50 61

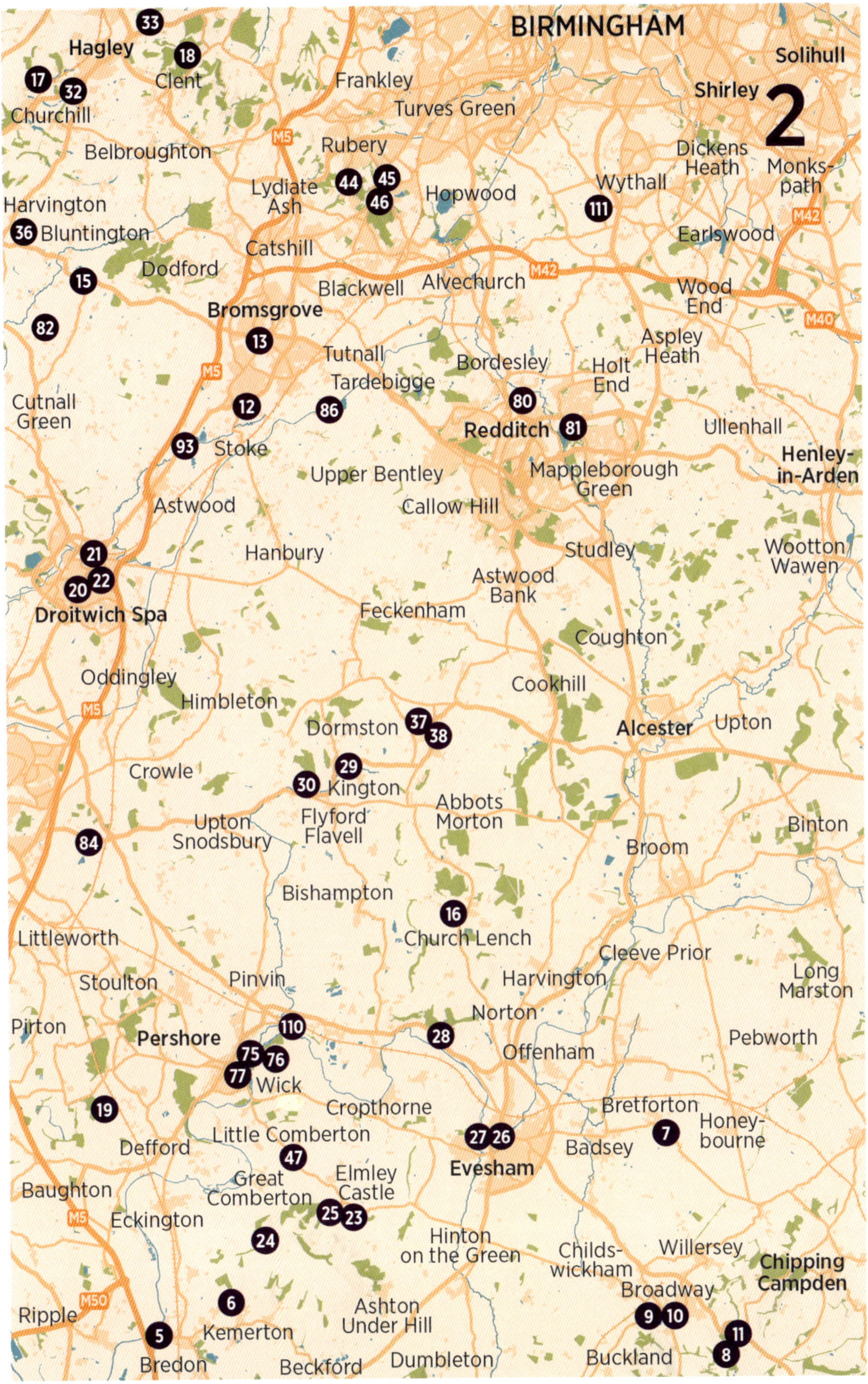
BIRMINGHAM
2
Solihull
Shirley
Hagley
Clent
Churchill
Frankley
Turves Green
Belbroughton
Rubery
Dickens Heath
Monks-path
Wythall
Lydiate Ash
Hopwood
Harvington
Bluntington
Catshill
Earlswood
Dodford
Blackwell
Alvechurch
Wood End
Bromsgrove
Aspley Heath
Tutnall
Bordesley
Holt End
Tardebigge
Cutnall Green
Redditch
Ullenhall
Stoke
Henley-in-Arden
Upper Bentley
Mappleborough Green
Astwood
Callow Hill
Studley
Hanbury
Wootton Wawen
Astwood Bank
Droitwich Spa
Feckenham
Coughton
Oddingley
Cookhill
Himbleton
Dormston
Alcester
Upton
Crowle
Kington
Abbots Morton
Upton Snodsbury
Flyford Flavell
Binton
Broom
Bishampton
Church Lench
Littleworth
Cleeve Prior
Long Marston
Stoulton
Pinvin
Harvington
Pirton
Norton
Pershore
Pebworth
Offenham
Wick
Cropthorne
Bretforton
Honey-bourne
Little Comberton
Badsey
Defford
Evesham
Great Comberton
Elmley Castle
Baughton
Eckington
Hinton on the Green
Childs-wickham
Willersey
Chipping Campden
Broadway
Ripple
Ashton Under Hill
Kemerton
Buckland
Bredon
Beckford
Dumbleton
M5
M42
M40
M50
33
18
17
32
44
45
46
111
36
15
82
13
80
12
86
81
93
21
22
20
37
38
29
30
84
16
110
28
75
76
77
19
27
26
7
47
25
23
24
6
9
10
11
5
8

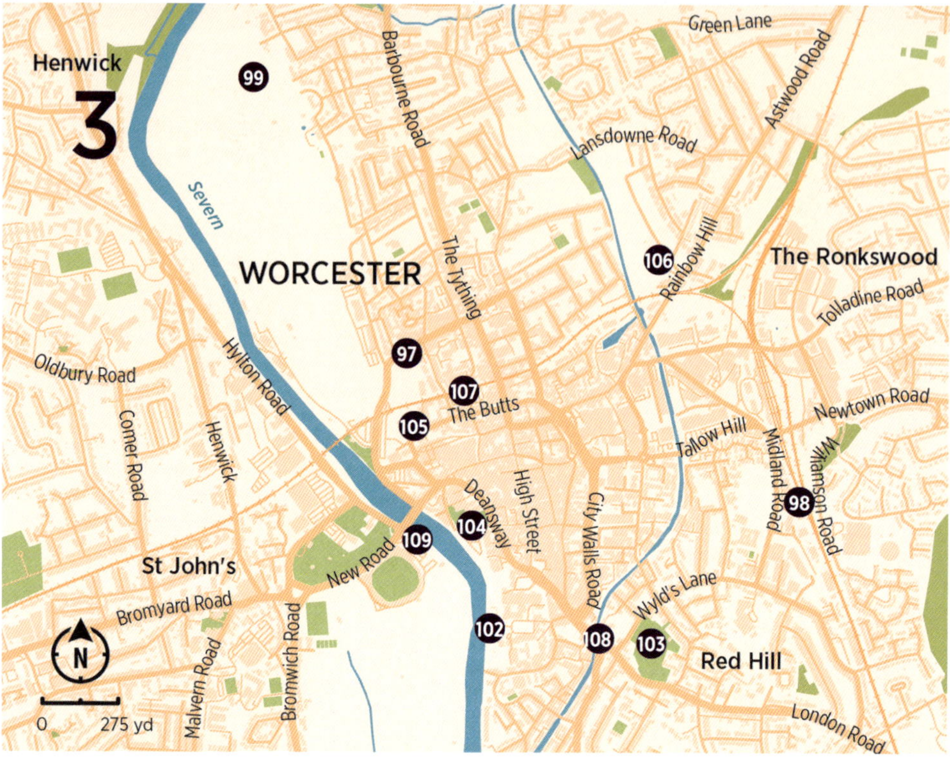
3
Henwick
99
Barbourne Road
Green Lane
Astwood Road
Lansdowne Road
Severn
WORCESTER
The Tything
106
Rainbow Hill
The Ronkswood
Tolladine Road
97
Oldbury Road
Hylton Road
107
The Butts
105
Newtown Road
Comer Road
Henwick
Tallow Hill
Midland Road
Williamson Road
98
Deansway
High Street
City Walls Road
104
109
St John's
New Road
Wyld's Lane
Bromyard Road
102
108
103
Red Hill
N
Malvern Road
Bromwich Road
London Road
0
275 yd

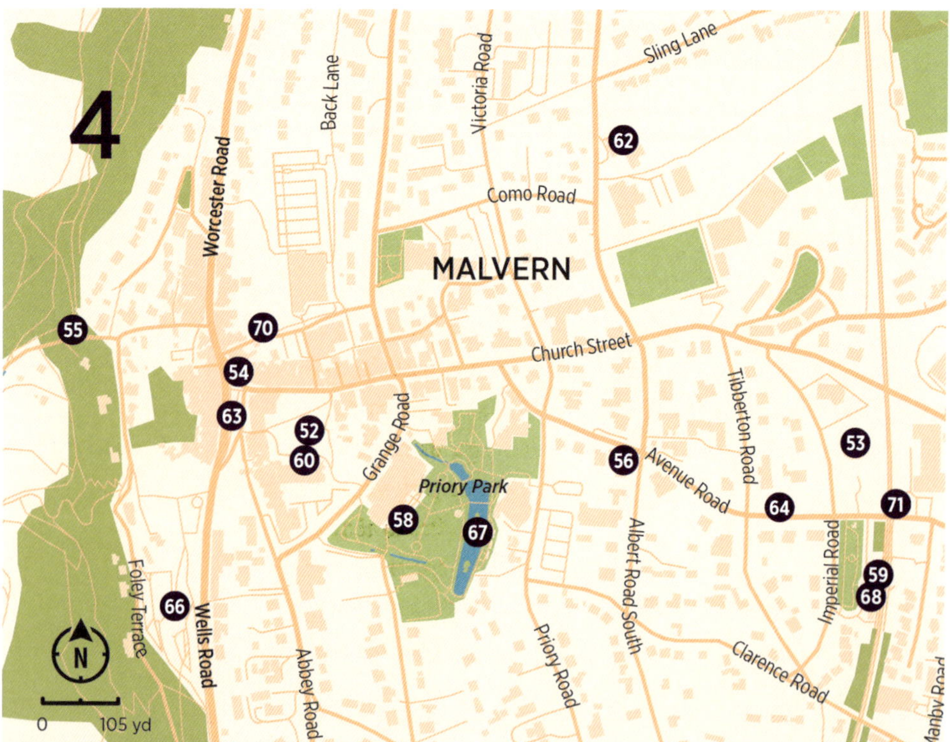
4
Sling Lane
Back Lane
Victoria Road
62
Worcester Road
Como Road
MALVERN
55
70
Church Street
54
63
52
60
Grange Road
56
Avenue Road
Tibberton Road
53
Priory Park
58
67
64
71
Albert Road South
Imperial Road
59
68
Foley Terrace
66
Wells Road
N
Abbey Road
Priory Road
Clarence Road
Manby Road
0
105 yd

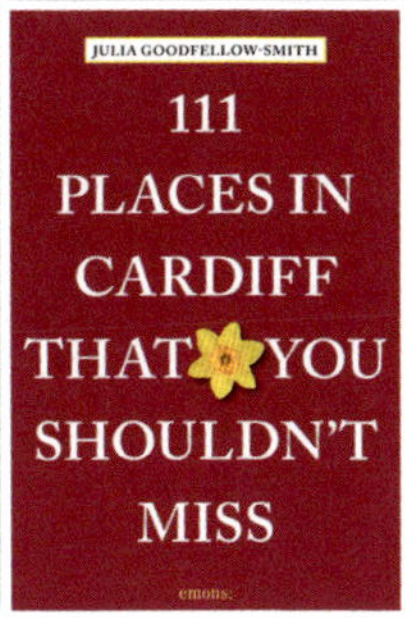

Julia Goodfellow-Smith
111 Places in Cardiff
That You Shouldn't Miss
ISBN 978-3-7408-2465-5

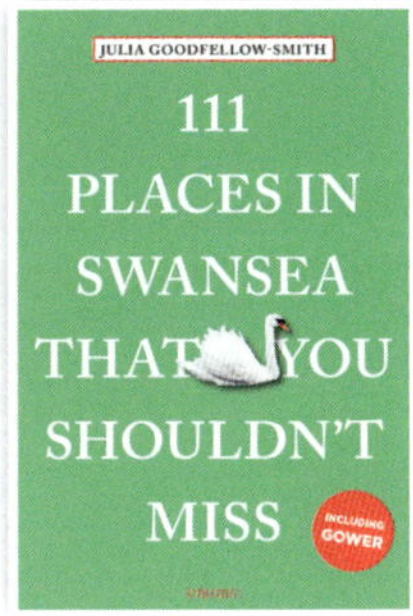

Julia Goodfellow-Smith
111 Places in Swansea
That You Shouldn't Miss
ISBN 978-3-7408-2065-7

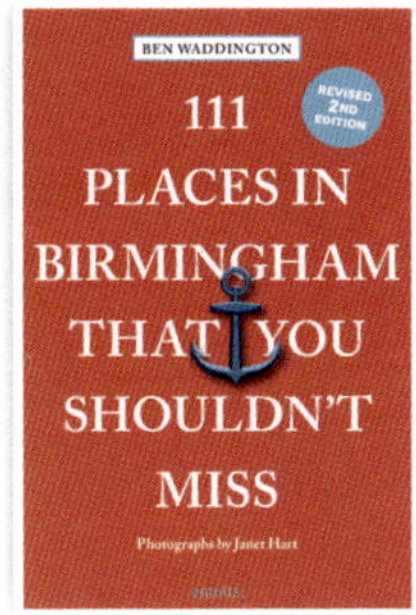

Ben Waddington, Janet Hart
111 Places in Birmingham
That You Shouldn't Miss
ISBN 978-3-7408-2268-2

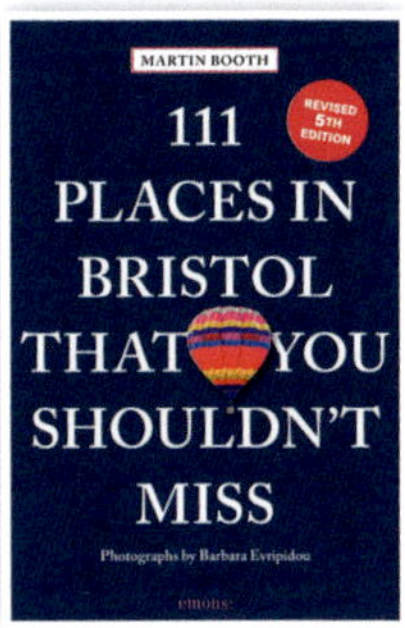

Martin Booth,
Barbara Evripidou
111 Places in Bristol
That You Shouldn't Miss
ISBN 978-3-7408-2512-6

Martin Booth,
Barbara Evripidou
111 Places for Kids in Bristol
That You Shouldn't Miss
ISBN 978-3-7408-1665-0

Martin Booth,
Barbara Evripidou
111 Places in Bath
That You Shouldn't Miss
ISBN 978-3-7408-2871-4

Phil Lee, Rachel Ghent
111 Places in Derby
That You Shouldn't Miss
ISBN 978-3-7408-2432-7

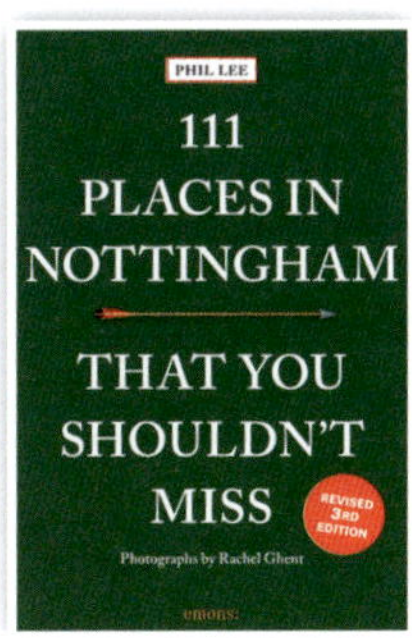

Phil Lee, Rachel Ghent
111 Places in Nottingham
That You Shouldn't Miss
ISBN 978-3-7408-2925-4

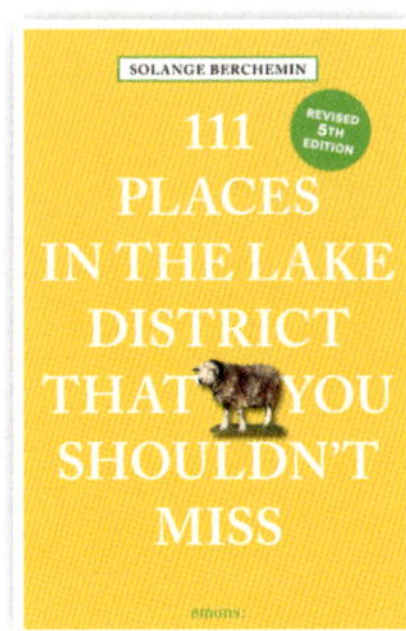

Solange Berchemin
111 Places in the Lake District
That You Shouldn't Miss
ISBN 978-3-7408-2824-0

Roly Smith, Chris Gilbert
111 Places in the Peak District
That You Shouldn't Miss
ISBN 978-3-7408-2551-5

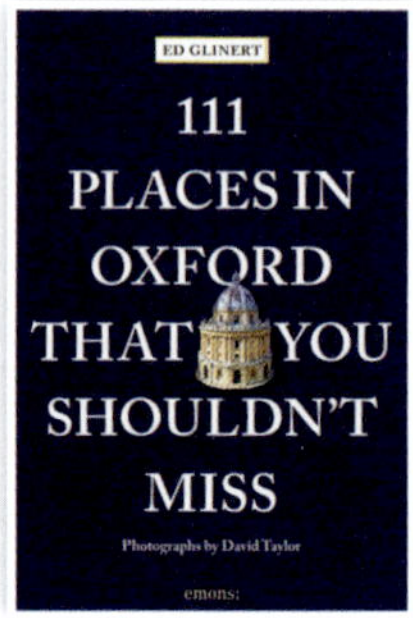

Ed Glinert, David Taylor
111 Places in Oxford
That You Shouldn't Miss
ISBN 978-3-7408-1990-3

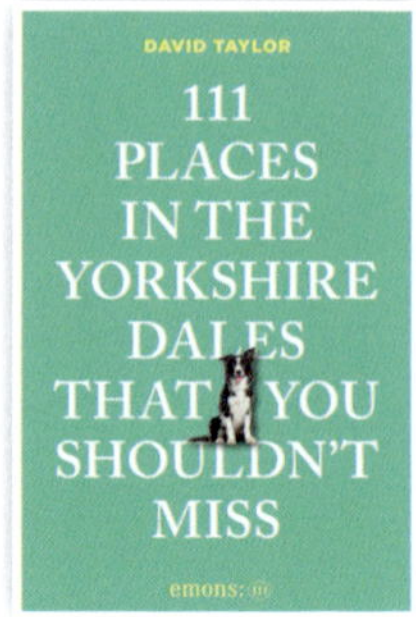

David Taylor
111 Places in the Yorkshire Dales
That You Shouldn't Miss
ISBN 978-3-7408-2792-2

Ed Glinert, David Taylor
111 Places in Yorkshire
That You Shouldn't Miss
ISBN 978-3-7408-1167-9

David Taylor
111 Places in Northumberland
That You Shouldn't Miss
ISBN 978-3-7408-2923-0

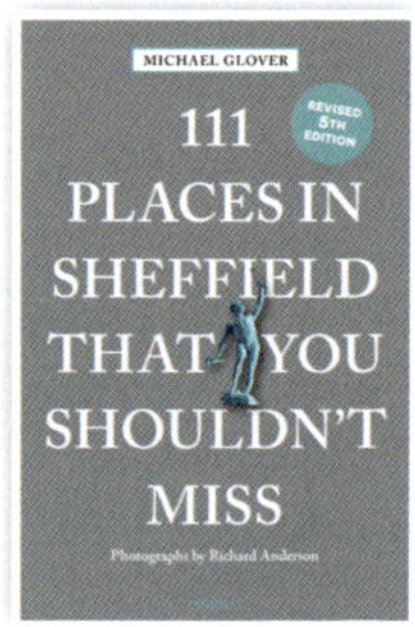

Michael Glover,
Richard Anderson
111 Places in Sheffield
That You Shouldn't Miss
ISBN 978-3-7408-2348-1

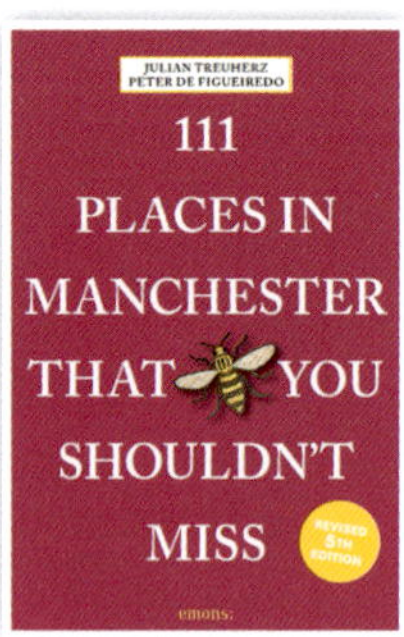

Julian Treuherz,
Peter de Figueiredo
111 Places in Manchester
That You Shouldn't Miss
ISBN 978-3-7408-2645-1

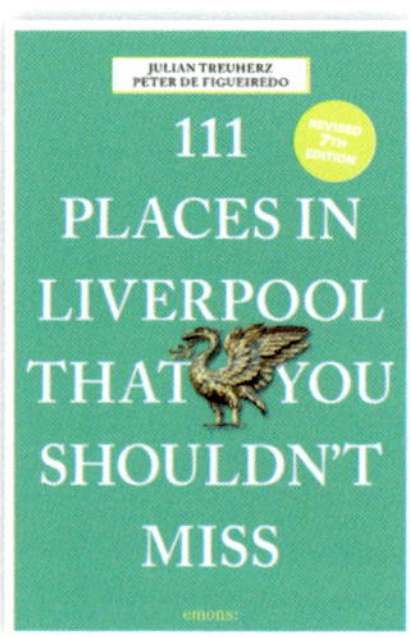

Julian Treuherz,
Peter de Figueiredo
111 Places in Liverpool
That You Shouldn't Miss
ISBN 978-3-7408-2515-7

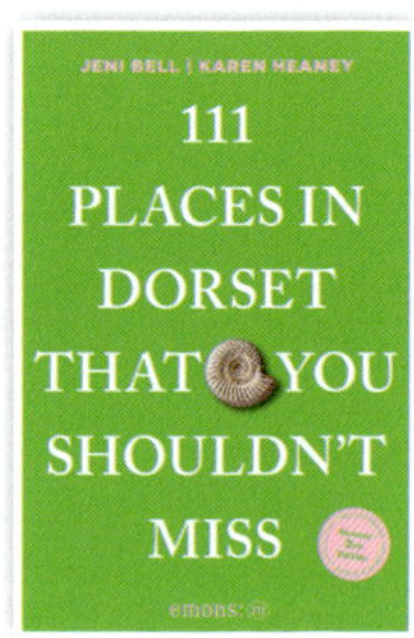

Karen Heaney, Jeni Bell
111 Places in Dorset
That You Shouldn't Miss
ISBN 978-3-7408-3018-2

ACKNOWLEDGEMENTS

This book has been a real team effort. First, my husband Mike helped with the research as well as the photography.

Friends and family have also contributed. Thank you, Sue, Alex, Simon, Jules and friends, Will, Sue and David, Hazel and Paul.

Then there are the tour guides, journalists, authors, librarians and venue managers who helped me with my research and photography. Thank you.

Much of the book's production happens behind the scenes at the publisher – Laura Olk, who commissioned me to write this and other *111 Places* books, Tania Taylor, who patiently queried and edited the manuscript, the proofreaders, photo editors, page formatters, marketers and anyone else I have unwittingly missed from the list – thank you.

THE AUTHOR

Julia Goodfellow-Smith loved living in Worcestershire. Dressed as a jellyfish, she walked the Malvern Hills during the COVID lockdown, and as lockdowns eased, she explored the rest of the county with her husband Mike. They have researched and photographed this book together, so they can share their love of this beautiful and important county with others.

The information in this book was accurate at the time of publication, but it may change at any time. Please confirm the details for the places you're planning to visit before you head out on your adventures.